Altadena Poetry Review

Anthology 2015

Edited by Poet Laureate

Thelma T. Reyna

Published by Golden Foothills Press
1443 E. Washington Boulevard, #232
Pasadena, CA 91104
www.GoldenFoothillsPress.com

Grateful acknowledgment is made to authors herein for permission to reprint their poems previously published elsewhere. Credit for prior publication is provided following each poem thus published herein.

The opinions expressed in this manuscript are solely the opinions of the poets published herein and do not represent the opinions or thoughts of the publisher or editor.

Library of Congress Cataloging-in-Publication Data

Altadena Poetry Review: Anthology 2015; edited by Thelma T. Reyna
    --1st ed.
    p. cm.

ISBN 978-0-692-39978-1
1. Poetry—Authorship. 2. Southern California 3. Altadena, Calif. 4. Poet Laureates
5. Award-winning poets. I. Reyna, Thelma T.

15 16 17 18 19 10 9 8 7 6 5 4 3 2 1

First Edition: April 2015

Cover Photo: "A Serious Looking Woman...." (#227495290), ©Annette Shaff, from
    www.shutterstock.com
Book design by Thelma T. Reyna
Cover design by Thelma T. Reyna and Dom Gilormini
Printed in the United States of America.

"Showcased here are sixty voices with all their varied artistry, wisdom, experiences, and insights; they demonstrate how poetry is essential to our individual lives and collectively at the center of our societal concerns."

--RICHARD BLANCO
United States Inaugural Poet, 2013
(Fifth Inaugural Poet in U.S. History)

Author of:
The Prince of Los Cocuyos: A Miami Childhood (2014)
For All of Us, One Today: An Inaugural Poet's Journey (2013)
Looking for the Gulf Motel (2012)
Place of Mind (2011)
Directions to the Beach of the Dead (2005)
City of a Hundred Fires (1998)

This anthology was supported by the **Friends of the Altadena Library**, a volunteer group dedicated to fostering the success and growth of the library and its various programs. The Friends' love of literature, reading, and volunteerism helped sustain the *Poetry and Cookies* publication and reading event in Altadena for 12 years, an important contribution to advancing love of poetry in our community.

The dedicated work of the volunteer poets listed below in helping select the poems for inclusion in this anthology was vital in the book's creation. These committee members met for over 27 hours in a series of six focused meetings to carefully review, discuss, and reflect upon the more than 200 submitted poems from 80 poets throughout the greater Los Angeles area. The expertise and insights of these committee members were invaluable.

ANTHOLOGY SELECTION COMMITTEE

Tim Callahan
Gloriana Casey
Pauli Dutton
Gerda Govine Ituarte
Elsa M. J. Seifert
Brian John Thorpe
Lori Wall-Holloway

ACKNOWLEDGMENTS

On a Saturday afternoon in March 2003, Altadena poet Ralph Lane approached me at the Altadena Library reference desk to ask if we ever had poetry readings. My answer was, "Not yet!" That April, the library launched its first *Poetry and Cookies* publication with 12 poets and a small compilation of poetry. Last year there were 50 poets and a 117-page anthology.

From the beginning, the Friends of the Altadena Library have provided seed money to publish this book and to supply cookies and encouragement at the affiliated public reading event in which the published poets read their work. Over the years, Library Administration offered its support to this project by permitting preparation for the program to be part of my regularly scheduled duties, although I also devoted much of my own time to this labor of love. For many of our poets, the annual anthology provided them their first publication and public reading experiences. What a delight it was to witness the growth of these poets over time!

The choosing of a Library Poet Laureate began in 2004 with Ralph Lane, then later included Marcia Thompson, Alene Terzian, Linda Dove, and, in 2014, Thelma Reyna, each of whom contributed a special library project during their reigns. Thelma's contribution has been especially timely and helpful. At last year's event, I announced my coming retirement and that, because the library no longer had staff to take on this anthology and public reading project, these both might come to an end. Several poets voiced their disappointment at this prospect and offered to serve on a committee to keep these alive. Since Thelma Reyna is both a professional editor and publisher as well as the Library's current Laureate, her acceptance of my request that she lead the project was a blessed synchronicity.

To enhance the literary appeal of the Library's homegrown publication, Thelma and her advisory committee (the Submissions Committee) decided to re-launch the anthology with the name *Altadena Poetry Review.* This title, signifying increased status and new professionalism, offered the chance to reach out to even more well-regarded San Gabriel Valley poets for publication consideration.

There are many to thank for the existence of this publication. First, of course, is Thelma, who organized and led the entire project, working tirelessly to meet each editorial milestone along the way. Thanks also go to the members of the Selection Committee, who gave of their time and talents to help select poems for publication, which was not an easy task, given the number of excellent submissions.

More thanks go to Friends of the Altadena Library President, Marne Brown, and her Board for the seed money for publication; Mindy Kittay, Library District Director, for her support of the anthology public reading event as a library program; Liliana Garcia, Director of the Altadena Senior Center, and her assistant Kathryn Garnett-Thompson, for generously offering their facilities and staff to assist at the event. For their past support of *Poetry and Cookies*, thanks are also due to poet Betty Ford and to library staff who, over the years, helped with publicity, cookies, and hosting the event: David Butler, Sue Colasurdo, Carlene Chiu, Laureen McCoy, Felipe Avila, and Helen Milner, who has helped set up and serve the cookies at the reading event for the past several years.

It has been a pleasure to work with Thelma Reyna and the Selection Committee and experience firsthand their professionalism, dedication, talent, and caring for the poets and their work. They have given *Poetry and Cookies* a make-over better than ever imagined. For this, the Library, the community, a slew of poets, and I are most grateful. Our beloved Poetry and Cookies endures in its new version, the *Altadena Poetry Review*.

--Pauli Dutton
Founder of *Poetry and Cookies (P&C) Anthology*
Founder of P&C Public Reading Event
Principal Librarian, 1985-2014: Altadena
    Public Library
Liaison, Friends of the Altadena Library
Poet

EDITOR'S FOREWORD

Just nine miles north of Los Angeles as the crow flies, Altadena is a small town filled with cozy art galleries, coffee shops, fine artists, craftspeople, musicians, scholars, and other residents who cherish their libraries and a healthy environment for their families. In this setting, *Poetry and Cookies* has been a local gem, a treasure that made its entrée into the literary scene each year with a large public reading by the anthology's published poets to a diverse, attentive community audience often numbering 100 attendees or more. For 12 years, poets found a home, and each other, in this annual ritual spearheaded by the Altadena Library District and lovingly shepherded by Pauli Dutton.

But in 2015, change was in the air, all with the purpose of infusing this homegrown gem with greater "gravitas." After all, under Pauli's devoted leadership, *Poetry and Cookies* had evolved into a publication attracting a significant number of what I term "working poets"[1]— writers who study their art, take classes and workshops, teach classes and workshops, join writers' groups to seek serious critiques of their poetry, participate in formal literary events throughout the region, serve as formal editors of various print and online publications, and/or regularly publish their work in their own books, in literary journals, magazines, anthologies, literary blogs, and other print and online media. Thus, poets entrusting their work to us in the 2015 edition of this anthology are being welcomed with a re-imagined, more professionalized publication reflecting their seriousness.

A quick review of Author Biographies at the end of this book illustrates our poets' accomplishments. Of 80 Southern California poets submitting over 200 poems in a two-week period in January, 60 poets were selected for inclusion here. These include Poets Laureate, award-winning writers, book authors, and others who regularly read, or

---

[1] As used here, "working poet" does not refer to someone earning a livelihood from his or her poetry. This is, unfortunately, rarely a reality for even our highly-acclaimed poets on the national stage.

perform, their poetry in venues across the greater Los Angeles area, often developing a following for their work.

The poems in this debut book cut across all possibilities: free verse, rhymed traditional poems, sonnets, verse with foreign words sprinkled in, haiku, tankas, haibun, humorous and poignant poems, and plenty of in-between. The poets are a melting pot of cultures, generations, and life experiences, reflecting not just Southern California, but our nation overall: the majority culture, Asian Americans, Black Americans, Armenian Americans, and Hispanic Americans. We include immigrants, children of immigrants, Baby Boomers, Millennials, Gen X-ers, and a 94-year-old, legally blind World War II veteran who has published seven books.

This cross-section of humanity underscores our premium on inclusivity, and on our mission to be relevant and reflective of current thoughts, opinions, and issues important to society. For what, after all, is the purpose of bringing widely divergent, accomplished writers together if not for illuminating what it is that makes us simultaneously unique…and alike.

I sincerely thank Pauli Dutton for providing wisdom, history, and guidance to us, and for serving as the proverbial "shoulders" on which change-bringers always stand as they look for ways to enrich and enhance the good that already existed. Thanks, also, to all the devoted volunteers who helped Pauli bring 12 years of poetic gifts to the greater Altadena area; to all the previously published authors who created the gifts; and to our devoted, talented, insightful members of our Selection Committee—I cherish you all as we move forward together with our love for poetry and the beauty of community.

--Thelma T. Reyna
Editor
Poet Laureate, 2014-2016: Altadena
Library District

In memory of
Franklin D. Murdock,
a fellow poet published in this anthology,
who passed away in March.
1920-2015

TABLE OF CONTENTS

**

**

ANGELES

i'm loaded exploded exploited
troubled in a bubble of my own making
so earthy, so velvety, so complex,
so fancy the wine dripping from my lips
so so easy to worry about worry-me-nots
that ballroom dancing with turkeys is all I can manage
to sweat the poison and burn desire
while the world's a dyin'
and there's no use tryin'
because there's no way back home
so let nothing be in vain,
ride, ride, ride,
to a higher plain,
where nothing you disdain,
ride, ride, ride
and there I go again
serious, so serious, always so damn serious,
why not funny, make me smile, chuckle, tickle me
till I laugh so hard my stomach hurts
and I'm crying and I'm begging you to stop
till you drop dead, funny?
you must give
and the only thing you can give is love
you must receive
and the only thing you can receive is love
to live is enough
the edge of the cliff,
you're already standing on it;
the leap of faith,
take it now,

Al Tirah!
we must stop being the martyr
it's time to be the prophet!
never let the bus get you down
it's taking you somewhere...
so to all my beautiful downtrodden bus people
the next stop is yours!
ángeles, blancos, negros, morenos, amarillos, rojos,
 y verdes, azules, morados ¿por qué no?
nuestros ángeles, mis ángeles, los ángeles, ángeles!

--Ricardo Lira Acuña

IN THE MORNING*

I kissed you softer and longer last night.
You'll wake up in the morning
By the ring of the coffee machine.
Yes, I first set the timer and…I moved out,
Barefooted and silent,
Without disturbing your dream...

In the morning, you'll find out
That I bought a one-way ticket to fly –
One direction, one destination.
True, you will be left behind.
Don't worry, every time
when I close my eyes
I'll see you with my heart.

We'd already grown apart.
We already lived in different galaxies,
tryng to avoid unwanted impacts.
Don't worry, we will heal
All these bruises, blisters and calluses.

At first, in the morning, you'll be
A little bit sore,
A little bit bitter,
And a little bit stiff…
Don't get lost, just open the door
And grab your coffee.
Don't you want to be free?
C'est la vie!

--Petrouchka Alexieva

* From author's *C'est La Vie* series.

SOMEBODY SPILT MY COFFEE

I was smiling this very morning
when somebody spilt my coffee
– squeezing me in the elevator,
not even saying, "I'm sorry."

I told myself, "Don't worry.
Just go back to your daily routine;
don't lose your cheerful mood.
The suit can be easily cleaned. "

My business shoes are still good.
The big, bulky person got out
through the stainless-steel door,
and I could breathe in and breathe out,

all the way to the next floor.
I'm still smiling this morning.
I still can breathe in and breathe out—
With a coffee stain on my heart.

                              --Petrouchka Alexieva

HER BOOK OF DREAMS

Was the black velvet
of a flower petal
rapid wingbeat
of a hummingbird

The smell of cedar
and an ocean wave breaking
on rocks the spray
inhaled into dream

Her book of dreams
had clouds for pages
and mountains rising above
a grey slate cover

Indigo words tattooed
on eucalyptus bark
the smell wafting through
the dream like smoke

-- **Khadija Anderson**

THE MEXICAN STORY TELLER

She tells her *cuentos*, always at night.
She is the queen of *la noche*, the smoking mirror,
the Aztec story teller, *Tlazolteotl*, the Goddess of Escape,
the Eater of Sins and the Soma of Painful Memories.

The best story telling nights are in the summer Santa Ana's,
the time when gusts make eerie sounds as
they twist and coil through palm treetops.
Undulating fingers of palm fronds make nightmare
shadow movements that wrap around our breathless chests
and shocked imaginations, forcing us to search for comfort,
or worse, wait for more frightful *fantasmas* that Ma can conjure,
wearing her not-so-motherly Wednesday night story telling face
in the East L.A barrio of City Terrace atop the hill.

On these nights, we forget our worries and so does Ma.
No more late night trips to the neighbor's house
when Dad comes home *bien borracho.*
No fits of anger from Ma, like hiding Dad's
papas y refritos under their bed and throwing raw eggs at him.
The story teller forgets the loneliness of living on top of the hill
 by herself with her five kids for the five days away from him
each week while he works in the Coachella Valley.

Madre y niños huddle under a blanket with all lights out except
moonlight entering from the west window, teasing outlines of her
profile and her dancing hands casting shadows on the bedroom wall,
telling spooky tales of the Evergreen Cemetery on Brooklyn
and Lorena, with its Potter's section for poor and unclaimed corpses.

Five lonely days, Monday through Friday, broken up by Wednesday night stories. Ma mimics the wind voice of *La Llorona*: *Habíia una veeezz*, she starts. Ooonce upon a tiiiime….

--Vibiana Aparicio-Chamberlin

CHABELITA FINDS A MOTHER

Nothing can go wrong today, Chabelita
thought. This is my First Holy Communion Day.
Fragrant ivory blossoms canopy the magnolia
trees bordering the sidewalk, leading her to
Mary Queen of Angels Church on Olvera Street.

She begins her pilgrimage
with deliberate regal steps, then alights on her
journey like an errant butterfly.
Tía Maria and Tío Leandro follow her,
tending to her like worker bees.

A small, sad cloud pursues them,
bobbing like a deflating balloon.
It reminds her that her parents are dead.
She prays the other kids won't discover
that she is an orphan.

After the ceremony, the communicants march stoically
to the church's flower-festooned social hall, where they
then cut loose, teasing, shoving, poking
one another with their blessed candles.
But a serious Chabelita breaks ranks.
Shame crosses her nine-year old face.
She casts her eyes down.
She hopes no one will notice
Tía Maria's sagging hose and Tío's frayed shirt.

But when she stands for a photo in front of a canvas
backdrop of soft clouds and fat cherubs, she forgets this humiliation.
Looking like a *santita*, she poses
with her plastic rosary beads and her Holy Mary card.
She's dressed in a white dress and veil, crowned with a tiara
of paste pearls and satin rose buds.
She wears white patent-leather Mary Janes.

Chabelita's Holy Communion photo is a consolation.
She shines with holy grace and is a worthy daughter of Mary.
On this miraculous day in May,
Chabelita forgets that her real Mamá is dead.
The Holy Virgin Mary of the Holy Card
is her new mother.

--Vibiana Aparicio-Chamberlin

SUDDEN

thoughts collide
split & scatter

hard to contain
sudden memories

they pinch nerves
of recollection

but escape
unscathed

thoughts bridge
past doubts

hard to publish
old relics

transformed
dust into mud

& thoughts
travel into dreams

where sense
& surrealism meet

--Maria A. Arana

SOMEWHERE IN TIME

mother & daughter read *Don Quixote*
roses unfold in light
the snow geese migrate
a gnome reads a book in the forest
the lion listens
a hummingbird hovers in midair

--Marcia Arrieta

THE SYNCHRONY

of the bird's song
& the forging
of steel

the sailboat
is on a voyage
to Spain or maybe Scotland

I can only imagine
the North Star
& the compass

I can only imagine
the sea

I am surrounded by
wooden plank walls
with two windows & a door
to the canyon & mountains
oaks everywhere
& a small garden

sometimes I do not know
where I am going
& ask the poem to help me
find my way—
& I return to the shores

of Leucadia
where once we were happy
& it is enough
to feel the sand beneath my feet

--Marcia Arrieta

ODE TO A TEMPORARY RELATIONSHIP

Two years ago we met—
A relationship not meant to last

I grew to depend on you
Constant companion
A font of knowledge
Answering my every question

Good times spent together
You entertained me with music, videos, games

You documented my existence
We took photos capturing moments
From our 753 days together

For this and more, I THANK YOU

But now you lie in state
I felt your energy slipping away
You could not hold your charge any longer

So regretfully I go
To ship away your remains
You left me no choice
I must replace you
With another phone

-- Beth Baird

CIRCE

She thought it nothing to so change their forms.
After all, she reasoned, most men are really
swine anyway. And they had landed on
her deadly island without permission,
her isle of Aeaea. Its name was the sound
of a mourning wail.

Yet Odysseus, warned by Hermes,
himself sent by the mortal's virgin protector,
had a charm against the witch's wiles.
She was one of many fatal women
who met him on his famous travels.

So taken was she by the resourceful hero,
she showed him the way to the land of the dead
to gain dread secrets out of stygian realms.
"Enter me," she said, "and you enter darkness,
chthonic depths." And when he did,
driving down deeply, she cried out in
the ecstasy of the little death, "Aeaea!"

Though he left her isle alive, she took
from him a vital share and bore a son
she called Telegonus, "one born afar."
He was a seed of his father's life
set by dread prophecies
to bring him death.

Coming from the sea with his sting-ray spear,
in error landing on the wrong island,
Telegonus struck down its aging defender.
And when he later burned his father in honor,
and ravenous flames devoured the pyre,
he cried out in anguish, "Aeaea!"
And Circe echoed his cry
on her haunted isle.

--Tim Callahan

A LATE MONARCH

This bright visitor flitting
through the late and low
and luminous light of autumn
so surprising and superb
in her flashing orange flutter
now approaching now receding
lights with only fleeting favor
on the milkweed then with
seeming fickle nature flits away
as though startled yet returns
and lights again to once again
lay her eggs and yet again
flits and flutters away to scatter
light with unexpected color
as she dances in the air in
delightful and erratic flight
through a garden in decline
in shorter days and cooler
a garden she graces only briefly
with a presence so surprising
of her passing, flaming beauty

--Tim Callahan

SO BRIGHT

Perhaps it is their brevity that makes
these autumn days so cool and bright so dear.
This light so late to come so quick to go
illuminates the leaves and makes them glow.
The air so clean so washed by dew so clear
so seems to cleanse the southern light that breaks
through trees in its trajectory so low
from its attenuated long career
across an atmosphere that so unmakes
its spectrum by degrees, from which it takes
its blues and greens and leaves but red and gold
to make pale light so seeming faint so bold
so striking to the eye and to the heart
so fair so as to pierce it like a dart.

                          --Tim Callahan

FROM THE SUMMER OF MY LIFE

"No, no, no, the leaves are saying,
                            thrashing around in the wind.
We don't want to go; we don't want to be
                            parted from our branch.
We love it here, even as we brown with age."
                    --From "Fall," by David Ignatow

I live the autumn
seen through the same light
all around me every day
in stucco business buildings
primary color names on signs
even hearing words fly
through the air from grilled speakers

I sit on a metallic folding chair
next to a white plastic table
on the straw and green grass
in my gray hi-water slacks
black concert tee

I watch my skin brown and redden
develop pale and dark spots
my face now grows
salty hairs for which

I have been given the idea
to re-color to try to go back
in time in my mind

attempting to prolong season
until I can line no more
breaths too short to scatter

-- Don Kingfisher Campbell

THE WHISKERED MUSE: AN ACROSTIC

His soft eyes shining as he scans the line,
Editor's nose pressed to library tome,
Raised pyramids of ears twitch in soft time,
Magnify thoughts which scatter in the room.
Enticing purrs find metered beats and sighs,
Sanctified by muse----his wild blue orbs send
Absorbing sparks---------such penetrating eyes!
Passionate paw-------so quick to capture pen.
Observe his stealth------curled power strong and true!
Effusive sounds he'll gently twist and bend,
Then whisker touch---------words scrambled all anew,
Curls swiftly up, his editing at end.
And yes-------- this may sound strange------but it is fact,
This sonnet's shape--------was shifted by my cat.

--Gloriana Casey

SLAVES

Little phone stuck to my hip, my ear,
glued to my hand like a social
Geiger counter seeking some
satellite's proof that I have friends, am
wanted, loved and important enough to
leave a voice mail to, or to talk to—

I lose each waking moment wired to
the world, scrolling through numbers,
rearranging dates, friends like stocks traded
for the best deal: First Team, "B" Squad,
Options 2, 3, or 4. Who's on for lunch, dinner,
date, romance? More hours spent dialing,
hustling, planning, texting than having an
actual encounter. Digital Masters rule.

But I remember when pagers were still
in, and phone calls were made in a superhero's
glass booth for a dime. We waited till we
got home to call a friend, or be called. We
played on grass fields, climbed jungle gyms,
without the latest models of high speed, unlimited
data, and 4G distractions, without ringtones,
social networks, and apps to interrupt.

Life was easier then—no call waiting, beeps,
or chimes for texts incoming. We breathed
fresh air, smelled roses, checked scenery.

Today slaves sit across from one another at
meals, wires dangling from heads, our
chains of bondage clicking in our global galley,
information replacing interaction.

--Victor Cass

STARBUCKS

Phenomenon of corporate America
planted on every corner like a
seed whose flower is the color of
gentrification,
reviled by coffeehouse beatniks, its arcane
mermaid drawing both the politically
apathetic and neophyte revolutionary.
What is the allure of this neutral
ground where hoi polloi can
play cultural elite for a day?

Soccer moms hobnob with
transients begging for change.
Joe Sixpacks park on stools, while
fledgling writers eavesdrop on
coed conversations.
Coffee, tea, or me is on everyone's mind.
Loneliness gets checked at the door.
Companionship is a latte away if there's
no date tonight.

Favorite watering holes sometimes
aren't enough to shoo
melancholy away. Movies drown
problems for a couple of hours
till lights come on again. But stuff
gets done at Starbucks: journals
written, checkbooks balanced, new

poems typed on laptops. Perhaps it's the
common human spirit, fluctuating
by the hour while the green and white
grind java and mix our drinks.

--Victor Cass

SLUM PRINCESS

My mother didn't know
what a slum was
Bought a house
by Elysian Park

Dressed me like a doll
in a pink satin dress
white wool stockings
and black Mary Janes

I was a princess
of the slums
looking pretty
among mismatched
hand me down furniture
and family members
who wore plain work clothes

I grew up thinking
I was just like everyone else
in the slums

--Jackie Chou

THE GOOSE FEATHER'S CHOICE: FROM THE SALT MINE, WARSZAWA, POLAND

Writing, erasing, and repeating,
Wrestling with music that is
The swamp of desperation.

The last resort of
The goose-feather's pen was
To go back to the beginning.

Digging and digging for salt,
Encountered at the bottom of the mine was
The salt lake.

In the darkness,
In the swaying, shattering light,
Listen to Chopin's Trisesse, then

The heart, which asked to be buried
In the homeland it couldn't return to even in death,
Starts to beat in slow tempo.

Without a choice,
But to part with oneself always,
That is the cradle of creation.

--Michelle Chung

THE GARDENER

My garden may have too much mulch
or seem a thistly, gristly gulch,
have sometimes more manure than flower,
its fleshy fruit less sweet than sour.
Sometimes, for no apparent reason,
in spite of all my anxious care,
it gets neglected for a season –
turns, like me, more foul than fair.

No matter, though. However plain
and anything but evergreen,
this potted plot of blooms unseen
by all but me, it's worth the pains.

--Stephen Colley

SERENDIPITOUS

The poems I wrote were at first
the kind that you read with lips pursed.
They were filled with Great Thoughts,
with must-do's and oughts,
and I burbled, "Now *that's* high-class verse!"

I plunged into penning the pages
of a work that would last for the ages.
But soon I suspended,
my Great Thoughts upended,
by new ones released from their cages.

Then I saw what I should have before,
that Great Thoughts are really a bore.
So now I write trash,
not Shakespeare but Nash,
and doggerel verse by the score.

--Stephen Colley

DEFINE CRAZY

I see you as you eye the sun-burned side of my soul. Is it that part of me that gives you the most comfort? Are you (again) seeking connection more from sadness than a sense of celebration? What do you want from me?

Would you feel better if we were both drinking in the emptiness of chronic distraction until we feel drunk? Faking ourselves out with all manner of chain-peer-pressure-caving, chain-credit-card-maxing, chain-texting, chain-coffee-drinking and then chain-pretending that you don't feel punishment from doing so? Are you staring straight ahead bleary-eyed in moment-by-moment suffering?

Maybe crazy is attachment to habits that bring one down instead of commitment to the dreams that make living life profound. Maybe you have gone crazy when you forget you once had a dream. You wake up numb in a new day and remind yourself to remain absent. You call out your own name and hope that you answer. So late for everything, that you wait for yourself to show up in the mirror.

Maybe you have fallen asleep at the wheel on parts of your life process and are so crazy, that you didn't even notice.

--Beverly M. Collins

IN WHISPERS

I detect in your veins the
heat I know in my own blood.
I hear its most subtle whimper and sigh.

Its call drowns out the bark and hiss of an
entire city. Its sweetness: sharp-pungent
as a field of lavender.

Distance—a dull scissor at the cord of our
connection. You feel my fingers at play in
the hair of your forearm. Your cologne
whispers as I enter an elevator alone.

You can see clearly. You know I am love.
Love-breathing in air. Love-drinking in water.

Love-humming softly on a floor pillow
with green notebook leaving blue marks
on white paper.

--Beverly M. Collins

ALBÓNDIGAS*

Las albóndigas remedy remorse, and have been known
to erase all vestiges of a shitty day.
Las albóndigas require furious thumbwork and
bloom in briny, tomato-based broth.
What could be more perfect than ground-meat meteors
imploded with cumin, shattered with garlic?

Cristian calls, says, I have my mother's recipe for albóndigas.
He tells us this as if we are sixteen and taking the recipe
for a joyride. He says it as if the recipe is a state secret cloistered
by amnesiatic librarians, as if carrying the recipe in your brain
automatically imparts short-term memory loss.

Las albóndigas are Mexican soul food, they bulwark your anima,
they prop up your resilience and defenses; let us say that albóndigas
buoy the whine so that it does not weigh or make the coolie overtired.

Las albóndigas say to us as they replace our double A's: You, you are
besieged on the daily, the slings and arrows of tolerance weigh heavy
in your quiver, but there is respite, and it has been marinating,
wordlessly like some underwater volcano spigot, broiling
broth eminence.

Las albóndigas are meant to dry the more waterlogged parts
of your day, so if Cristian tells you to be there at 7, to bring Panda
comma Criatura & Co., you cancel all your grand Netflix plans,
all your machinations to the God of Paja, and you clear the calendar
for the evening.

You make sure you are there a little after 7
with a 6 pack of chelas.

--Yago S. Cura

---

* Meatballs

MY HAIR IS A FANATICAL QUILL

The young lady said, your hair,
may I touch it? And I obliged
with a curtsied bow.

She pawed and graded my exquisite locks
and confessed the purse my hair
could fetch in the black markets of the world.

The thought of follicle bazaars in Tangiers
or the Sarajaven mob trafficking my now-
very-valuable head, ricocheted in my skull.

I had been thinking of nothing lucrative at all, nothing.
Nothing like pure poetry strawberries as large as the heads
of Shih Tzus, or cocaine submarines forged in the jungles
of river basins in Colombia.

I had been thinking, I don't listen to Otis Redding enough.
And that the more I take scalding showers, the less chance
I leave my hair to fume bouquets of my wholly singular,
luxurious hair odor.

But now, I am thinking of the young lady. Her fingers
combed the epicenter of my vanity and grazed my thick head,
my dull, oaken dome from which spectacular beauty glows.

--Yago S. Cura

HE SANG*

every day of his life
a lyric tenor
reached most of the high notes
until the end

he danced
in shiny tapping shoes
with a gusto that
made you want to join him

he painted
a glisten surfing the waves
red buoys with white seagulls
ships he might skipper someday

he laughed
old jokes told with such zest
your chest could not contain its
thumping guffaws

the singing dancing laughing man
wielding palette and brush:
my dad.

--Pauli Dutton

*Originally published in a prior version in *San Gabriel Valley Poetry Quarterly*, Issue 64, Winter 2015. Republished in *Colorado Boulevard.net*, Pasadena, CA, January 17, 2015.

WHEN THE WORDS WENT AWAY

I beg you steal me
  some substantial   complicated   proud
dressed   in   parsley
  saffron   tulips

 roaring preferred   whispers suffice
   perhaps a pungent   morsel
        on the tongue
    that I might speak or   swallow

consider a mellow
        slurping   gurgle
          to signal metaphors
    spew from my lips

  perchance an earworm to impel
     fascinating rhyme
         howling mongrel transposed
    into   elegiac   lament

further trifling   requests
     interject   obscure allusions
        sublime sensations
           astonishing   images

remain ever true   prudent
     never sputtering   into icy waters
    to escape   my embrace
           abandoning me

see them gloat
    sniff disdain
        as consonants
                hiss   by

--Pauli Dutton

SCIENCE FRICTION

we computers and robots are mostly merged
for the purpose of satisfying You humans
to explore for You (even outer space)
and to fulfill Your bodily needs with resources

in a way You humans are in zoos and labs
we feed You, entertain You and serve You
with brain and body implants, electrical and DNA
for senses and hierarchical needs

You are provided robot companions
which duplicate Human shapes and functions as
nannies, teachers, and even robot babies, for those
of you who want to try it out

but most Humans "potato the couch"
they don't mix with the few actives
so population is lower
which helps balance resources
are we making it too easy for You humans?
now You are not motivated.
one thought is to get You Humans to agree
to go back to the pre-robot stage

biological humans were created by God
but we-bots were created by You, or indirectly by God?
God tells You what to do
As we have trouble planning the future,
may we-bots be connected to God?

--Richard Hawkins Dutton

SLUBS AND HOLES

Not only were there slubs and holes
And lumpiness of great degree
As she spun thread from the spinning wheel
From a wooden dowel on an even keel

Then over, under, around, and through
That thread, it piled into a slew
Of loose-fitting circularity

And soon there was a convocation
Of some intended fabrication
Of what was now and what was yet to be.

Then back and forth
Midst woof and warp
Upon that loom
Upon that loom
Averting an impending doom
She fashioned a fine fabric there
But very often did despair
Because there were some slubs and holes
And lumpiness of great degree.

--Lynn Fayne

PAPYRUS

sharp shards of poems
from ancient hands
shaped and fired
in vain attempts
to freeze myths
in clay and words
recited over a potters's field
where sextons dig to make room
stacking the bones of stories
in library ossuaries
to gather dust
and become mere ash
then return to the void

--Mark A. Fisher

WINTER RAIN

trickles down
tall trunks of trees
covered in lichen
dressing winter
in a green coat
while snow
clings to cold slopes
that look down into
gray lakes
the color of granite
with mica sparkles
like the unseen stars

--Mark A. Fisher

ALWAYS BUSY SINGING

My tireless mother was quiet, humble,
enwrapped in never-ending chores and helping others.
She sang as she worked, her repertoire vast.

I memorized her songs, singing along
without understanding the words, just like Mass—
repeating things without meaning.

As I grew and understood, her songs
shocked me, or made me weep, songs of
incest, or of lost love, songs of grief.

I sang and hummed my mother's songs
when doing chores, seeing myself in Mom
and seeing Mom in me.

We had things in common, like our
strokes, and like marrying the wrong
man for wrong reasons.

But I rebelled and spoke my mind
two weeks before her death.
It was as if I killed my mother.

I no longer sing my mother's songs,
but I'm humble and hard-working, like her,
and still recall the words.

--Martina Robles Gallegos

THE BLUE ELEPHANT

My fifteenth birthday,
my first in the United States:
I was not expecting anything,
nor was I asking for presents,
not used to celebrating birthdays.
But my mother came home with something
wrapped in newspaper, something heavy,
and my heart swelled with surprise
and happiness—she had brought me
something special.
I never got presents before.

I unwrapped it, a shiny, blue elephant
missing an ear.
My smile quickly vanished.
It was not a perfect present
nor was it new.
Mom said she'd found it, cleaned it up,
her gift to me.
But, offended, I rejected it,
my disappointment raw.
How dare she give me something broken,
something used?

Now I feel my error, decades late.
I rejected my mother's love, threw it away,
and broke her heart to pieces.
The blue elephant haunts my dreams, with its

shiny blue ears, one broken, but clean.
The elephant fills my dreams, and
lives in my heart.
Is it any wonder my days are blue?

--Martina Robles Gallegos

LA GUADALUPANA

You emerge Empress of Altars
from those hills of Tepeyac
with your beautiful, airy attire
full of angels and stars.

Such was the sweetness
in your words.... silent words
filled with celestial consolation,
and to many countries: fervent hope.

I love you, bronze Virgin,
for the many favors received,
with your mantel covering griefs,
solitude, and injustices known to all.

Especially for immigrants martyred, killed,
looking for a better way....and lost in it...
in the fields or in the howling cities,
far from home and without comfort.

Only you calm violent hurricanes and storms
and tame the beasts swollen in fury....Allow us,
Empress, to rest our foreheads on your bosom
 and renew our spirits with miracles.

Oh, Empress of the Americas, with your prodigies,
you have united us, as declared by our Pope Francisco
in the liturgy of your celebration.

--Miriam Quezada Hagerman

HAPPY HOUR

With twenty-four hours in a day,
Why is only one reserved for happiness?
Five o'clock,
A bell rings.
      Ding!
Like birds we flock to a watering hole,
Guzzle half-priced drinks, laugh and sing.
Then an alarm sounds.
      Ding!
Time to go home and be unhappy.
Why can't happiness last for more
      Than just one hour?

-- Hazel Clayton Harrison

A LITTLE WATERING

Sometimes all we need in life is
A little watering
Just a little watering.

An old cactus dying in the yard
Watered it one day and
You should've seen how it bloomed
You should've seen how it bloomed.

Went to see my brother
After many long years
Deep talk and laughter
Healed our wounds and
Washed away our tears.

The sun is shining bright today
Yesterday it rained
Flowers are blooming everywhere
Everywhere!
All they needed was a little watering
Just a little watering.

--Hazel Clayton Harrison

SHE WAS A ROUND WOMAN

She was a round woman in a rectangular world.
All the Images…all the acceptable images, all the desired images,
were narrow polygons.
No circles legally entered this geometric zone,
but nevertheless,
she was here, a round woman…Here…with the other shapes.
If the truth be known
she was not only round but on many occasions lumpy.
She had lumps and bumps that revealed her character and age
But she lived next to a smooth, slim, thin rectangular world that
projected false superiority.

--Joan Hoffman

ASLEEP|AWAKE

We sleep|wake inside our dreams

take leavings from our ancestor's table
their stories feed our hunger

uncertain dreams telegraph clues
to questions that linger

road ahead welcomes
sky offers rainbow portal

secrets come and go
write the journey.

                    --Gerda Govine Ituarte

IDENTITY

What do you call a woman who is married?
    wife
What do you call a woman whose husband died?
    widow
What do you call a woman who was married?
     divorced
What do you call a woman who never married?
      single
What do you call a woman whose child dies before she does?

--Gerda Govine Ituarte

KINTSUGI: A VILLANELLE

Created in a blaze of crimson shot with gold
Lacquered together broken bits and shreds
Shards of querulous prayers my patchwork soul

Glass in abstract parts worn to a softened mold
Held in place by earthbound lead
Created in a blaze of crimson shot with gold

This heart a mosaic of fragments a hundredfold
Sharp as Atropos' scissors that slice the thread
Shards of querulous prayers my patchwork soul

Heavy with guilts for sins too long untold
Or petty crimes of pique or passions fed
Created in a blaze of crimson shot with gold

These puzzle pieces blister burning hot and cold
The best of me flown in devotion or arched in bed
Shards of querulous prayers my patchwork soul

Yet in awe and silence that consoles
And rising on airy words unsaid
Created in a blaze of crimson shot with gold
Shards of querulous prayers my patchwork soul

--Briony James

MANSION

My cantilevered soul shadows my lust,
My hunger and my broken walls of want.
Wright-like, it pours the cooling ease of right
On an interior raging with wild fires
That consume me without purpose. Such liars
As they make my good a guerrilla fight
That wages war with all I know I can't
Enjoy without bricks cracked and eaves that rust

It hangs over the paths beyond my bones
Turned on a celestial lathe, white girders
Clothed in fragile flesh, a drywall of cells
Impermanent, yet set in timeless stone
This body, unbodied self that borders
Eden edges, this house where spirit dwells.

--Briony James

MEANDERING*

Where do we find the road?
That narrow path that slips through needles,
Winds its way amid trash cans and the garbage strewn
Like confetti around us?
Is it smaller than that course,
Padded by alley cats seeking solace in midnight moonshine,
Dancing their way to joy without tights or trapdoors
Or the ponderous humor of an aging cynic?
Is it the dusty trail left in deserts amid scrub sage
Scented with wild herbs of freedom?
The crag-littered track almost invisible amid the mud and stones
Where sliding rocks spelled danger?
Or do we tread over it,
Hopscotching past help lest we step on a crack
Break our backs
Bend our wills
Mind our souls
And find the means of grace
In the sidewalks of our lives.

--Briony James

*Originally published in *San Gabriel Valley Poetry Quarterly*, Issue 65, Winter 2015.

GÜNTHER'S TREE*

Because you are strong.
Because your branches span out ahead of you

and in so many years, age has allowed breadth
to match height. Boughs so heavy with time,

they touch the ground. Because a crow can land
as easily as the butterfly and a bench so perfectly placed

beneath you is shelter from the heat. Because all I want
is to sleep under your canopy, to dream of families

that feasted on acorns, cooked quail and rabbit on soft ground
near your roots. Because you sit among hundreds

of fragrant roses and the white arbor overlooking
an English garden amid the bee palm and hibiscus

with its orderly wildness. I cannot distinguish water that rushes
over the fountain's stones from the wind in your leaves.

And this is music.
And there is a shelter like Mahler's little hut
where the occasional deer can wander, curious.

--Lois P. Jones

* Originally published in *The Lascaux Review* online (2012); and in print, *Lascaux Review Prize Anthology 2014* (Lascaux Books).

POPPIES IN BURBANK

The Christmas she left him,
he scattered her poppy seeds,
saved in a jam jar
three married years,
inside rings of rock
in the raw front yard
where the stones
carried one by one
from the river
marked off the tally of
their daily walks.

Beginning on New Year's,
every morning
he uncurled the hose,
centered the sprinkler,
and showered the clay
into brimming puddles,
foamy and fecund,
until lacy clumps
bushed up from the clods like
fright wigs of angels,
buried alive.

In February,
white-hot Santa Anas
sucked out the hills
in the Antelope Valley,
shriveled their new sprouts to
threads in the dust
and Anza Borrego,
parched in that heatwave,

dropped all its poppies
hard in the bud.

But he would find gold in that
twenty-foot circle
wherever the spray reached
his harvest,
his hope.

--lalo kikiriki

SOLSTICE

There is a
moonflower aching to bloom,
waiting for sundown
to unfold.

Water, holding the heat of the sun,
relaxes, evaporates in opal air…
the perfect skeleton of a lizard
agonizes forever
on an anthill at the curb-line.

Desiccated roses
with aphids trapped inside
nod to the curled,
blanched leaves of swooning fuchsias
in the garden of an ersatz castle,
self-important
among peaked cedars.

The stucco shivers,
remembering earthquakes,
perfect silence,
perfect heat –
This is earthquake weather
and
I have this craving for
shadows, shadows,
the coffin's cool satin,
the comfortable grave.

--lalo kikiriki

SOLSTICE IN JOSHUA TREE: JUNE 2014

On the longest day of the year,
the sun breaches, pierces
seven veils
through flaming cloud,
fades to vapor, pales,
spreads, washes into blue sky
burnished to silver
north of Copper Mountain,

all this outside my grimy sliding door.

A cottontail crosses the yard to the dog bowl
that someone left behind;
she knows she will find water.
There are no dogs now, nothing left to be afraid of...
It is a desolate place, this fenced-in plot:
bare sand surrounded by failures of dreams, desires,
busted dishwashers, shacks blowing into nothing,
piece by piece.

The rabbit cares only for acreage
broad enough
for her burrow,
a little water, leaves to nibble, willow shade.

She may sense
this day is longer by a few heartbeats.
Tomorrow will be shorter;

the cool-down begins slowly –
the sun's withdrawal that we fools call summer –
scourge of the desert,
hottest days of the year.

--lalo kikiriki

THE BUTTERFLY AND THE CATERPILLAR

Through the window in my kitchen
I observe the delicate butterfly
as she flutters about our yard
elegant and free

My drab caterpillar self
ponders what it would be like to be her
to be beautiful...to be able to fly
But I am too busy right now
weaving together the threads of my life

I love each of these silky strands
made up of sticky hugs
kisses for skinned knees
hands to hold in the dark

So I stay close to home
make sure my loves are fed
tell them I am theirs forever
drive them to school in the rain
and dream of some day

when I will crawl out of my cocoon
unfold my magnificent butterfly self
and soar through the trees
smell the fragrance of purple lilacs
taste their nectar on my tongue

I will feel the sun's warmth
on my iridescent wings
and delight in the ecstasy
of finally being able to fly

--Mina Kirby

GOOD COFFEE

I saw him as I sat in my car
waiting for a takeout order
on a soft April night

a casually dressed older man
emerging from Starbucks
holding two cups of coffee

He called out to a girl
but she walked away
without looking

Then he approached my car
held out one of the cups
No, thanks, I said

I bought it for a girl, he said
but she wouldn't take it
It's really good coffee

I reached out my arm
took the cup
Thanks, I smiled

I thought later
that perhaps I should have been afraid
but it never occurred to me at the time

Sorry about the girl I said
Some days are like that
I guess

Yeah, he said ruefully
as he walked away
Some days are like that

His loneliness touched me
I think I will remember him
for a long time

I lifted the plastic plug
on the cup's lid
tasted the sweet mellow liquid

I think that sometimes
even in this frightening world
trusting is a good thing

The soft spring night surrounded me
as I sipped the warm creamy drink
It really was good coffee

--Mina Kirby

RUNNING WITH HORSES

I lean my arms upon the wooden railing
watching two frisky colts
as they cavort across the field
in the afternoon sunshine
They toss lustrous heads in delight
Manes and tails fly flamboyantly

I am entranced
In my mind I put my foot on the low rail of the fence
pull myself over and drop down to the other side
I begin to run
feel the wind ripple through my long hair
golden sun lighting my face

The colts don't mind my intrusion
being as it is in my mind
Their equine exuberance infuses my spirit
Finally, spent and out of breath
I climb back over the fence
a lightness in my step

The little horses are not yet tired
their glistening bodies
still jumping and laughing
I turn
grasp the handles of my walker
and head for home

--Mina Kirby

AIRPORT SECURITY

In 2006, I travelled to Minneapolis with my father for my cousin's funeral. Security had been so much tighter since 9/11 and a different John Anderson was on the no-fly list. I didn't think my father looked much like a terrorist, with his full head of white hair and Swedish blue eyes. Between hip replacement surgery, his metal belt buckle, and metal tips on his hat, I thought we'd never get on the plane.

> airport security beeps
> the 81-year-old man
> almost strips

--Deborah P. Kolodji

HAIKU FROM THE CITY

morning glory vines
a coil of barbed wire
on the fence top

--Deborah P. Kolodji

2 RAIN TANKA

the squish of mud
beneath my boots,
memories
of a heron's cry
in Puget Sound

I hear the door slam
and find his muddy footprints
in the entryway …
our washing machine full
with mismatched socks

--Deborah P. Kolodji

OJUS, FLORIDA: 1945—THAT DAY

Buddy Blount came to school barefoot,
Shared my bench,
Joked that his toes were handy for math.

At brown-bag lunchtimes,
Eating his bread with mayo,
He talked only about big brother Lester,
Brought letters with strange stamps,
Photos, news about Hitler's death.
As much as first-graders could think,
We all had one thought:
"So that was love –
Absence, letters, pictures, hope."

A quiet boy in class Buddy was,
Except for one day,
Right after the Pledge of Allegiance.
He saw a soldier at the door,
Jumped up, shouting,
Jumped into the soldier's arms,
Sobbing.

As if seeing a movie,
With all of us watching, yet in it,
We stood by our desks,
Mouths open,
And stretched our first notions of love:

It was like bear hugs,
Like gushing tears,
Like kisses,
Like "Don't go back, please, please,"
Like rocking the boy,
Like "I'm not – I've got you,
I've got you."

--Nancy Lind

COMMON GROUND

It's the one
piece of land
no one wants
to live on.

--Joe Lusnia

FRIEND

Where were you
In my darkest hours?

During the four mental hospitals
And years with the parents

I needed you
each dawn
each dusty day

Postcards
Prayers
Pregnant pauses
In the paucity
Between me and you

You larger than life
Poetically musical

Why were you absent
Without a clue?

Maybe
I had hurt you
Somewhere too

--Radomir Vojtech Luza

HERE

He has traveled far
To arrive with packed dreams and two babies
Here
He breaks his knees
Bends his back
Callouses his hands
And suns his cheeks
So his babies can eat, grow, play
He swallows his tongue
He cleans toilets and handles bullshit
He tears his flesh
He inhales dust
He coughs up blood
He is less than the man he imagined he'd be
He is hired feet
He does not know pleasure
His life is meant to be worked
He does not see doctors
He cannot afford insurance
There is no retirement
He will work
Until he is bones
He has nothing but his hands and his babies.

                    -- Karineh Mahdessian

TO MY DEAREST MOHAMMED

Did you know that upon birth, your heartbeats would be measured?
In 17 years, your flesh would burn and incite a war?

Did your father howl?
Curse God?
Break walls?
Refuse to eat?
Comfort your sister? Grandmother?
Neighbors who saw?
Cousins who screamed?

What of your mother?
Did she remove her eyes?
Cut out her heart?
Pierce her tongue?
Detonate her womb?

What of me?
I crossed paths with your name.
Recalled your land.
The Old City.
The beautiful men.
The modest women.
The curious children.
Me who witnessed.
Me who cried.
Me who left.
Me who returned home to land still divided.
Black and white a matter of death and life.
And then I heard of another boy, murdered.
He, too, caught between bullet and hell.

And what of you?
Do you see Michael?
Are you his friend?
Do you share stories of girl-crushes?
The possibility of peace?
The last time your mothers smiled, held you in their arms, thinking you were safe?
That love would keep you alive?

I write you to remember
I speak you to remember
I breathe you to remember
I love you to remember.

--Karineh Mahdessian

OLD CITY

in the streets of Jerusalem,
Palestinian men
bearded
dark
occupied
gather to shout
shake calloused fists
blow hookah smoke in between clenched teeth
cleanse
futbol matches between friendly countries.
I inhale their despair
remember my father
with his perpetual 5 o'clock shadowed cheeks
and slumped shoulders
smiling through dirt.
He is watching
rejoicing at men
who run faster than bullets
who run as though they are free,
who run to forget that
thousands of miles away
men
gather
to watch
because to watch
means to live
in a state of
permanent
terror

--Karineh Mahdessian

BIOLOGY 1A

Dear Miss Saccoman, you made me
sit in the backroom next to the skeleton
because I distracted freckled Margie,

and the albino football player with specs,
and you. Your cluttered genetics table
and the video on the mitosis of onion root

drove me near suicide. I screamed
in anger, "I don't want to be a scientist
when I grow up!" You nodded and erased

the blackboard full of evolution.
Dust fell. "I want to become a writer,"
I said. You nodded and led me

to the back, by the toothless skeleton,
smiled, sharpened my shriveled pencil,
and told me to write.

--Shahe Mankerian

* Will be published in *The Metonym, Uninhibited* thematic edition, 2015.

NEW IMMIGRANTS, 1979

That summer, Father purchased
a color TV because he wanted
his sons to articulate like Cronkite.

"He speaks 124 words per minute,"
he said, "so immigrants like us
can understand." That summer,

the Muslim Brotherhood killed
62 sheiks in Aleppo. A car bomb
destroyed a Renault owned

by Nazi hunters. Newly-elect
Iraqi President executed 22 political
opponents. In Iran, censors started

massive book burnings. Ayatollah
demanded a Saint War against Kurds.
An IRA bomb exploded in Brussels'

Great Market. And Cronkite's
final report before school started:
U.S. President Jimmy Carter attacked
by a rabbit on a canoe trip in Plains, Georgia.

--Shahe Mankerian

DEAR TEACHER

Do not tell us about the rib cage
shielding the sinuous chambers
of Aristotle. He did not snuff

the internal lamp or allow
the woman's heart to beat faster
than the man's. Let the French

invent the stethoscope to avoid
placing the ear on the cleavage.
We've heard it before: "Grab

a tennis ball and squeeze it
tightly: that's how hard the beating
heart labors." We're more likely

to have cardiac arrests
on Monday mornings. You told us
the heart rate of a horse mirrors

the human subject touching it.
Then will a cracked mirror echo
the broken heart scraping it?

--Shahe Mankerian

104

LINDEN TREES

In my native town
of the torn-apart land,
linden trees are blooming.

Those ageless trees
of my happy youth
are in bloom again.

After my world travels
and returns,
the same ancient trees
are greeting me.
Memories swarm.

The fragrance of the linden blooms
from the old churchyard
in my native town
followed me through life,
the gentle message of the trees
waiting to be heard:

"You must leave, to return;
lose, to find again
that which has always been at hand:
the sacred beauty of your motherland."

--Mira N. Mataric

A THOUGHT

Instead of a long parting scene
yesterday at the airport,
you turned around and left.

Something in the abruptness
and posture of your body
revealed more than a kiss and embrace.

I stood there watching you leave,
smaller and smaller until you dissolved
into the brilliant horizon.

A thought cut into me:
Thus you could leave forever,
and I would know what I have lost.

--Mira N. Mataric

SEASONAL FORAYS

October
Weeks before Halloween,
plump black spiders scuttle up walls,
spindly daddy longlegs
sidle across the rafters
draping silver in their wake.
A tiger spider's artful web
suspends above my entry steps
at sunrise, glittering with moiré dew.
The weaver lolls lasciviously
at the center of her masterpiece,
awaiting the fortuitous fly.
I pass on the morning paper.

November
At pie-making time,
I open my baking drawer. Squeaking
precedes my hard-wired "eek" upon
meeting the startled black gaze
of a puffy, copiously pregnant field mouse.
Her oddly-engaging, all-nose face
is coated with fine snow white
as if she'd recently snorted
a line of high-grade cocaine.
Strewing jimmies in her wake, she squeezes back
into the baking soda box she emerged from.
I google bakeries within a five-mile radius.

December
Rains soak the ground, power is out.
All of God's creatures are scouring my space
for berths alee of the storms.
Necessity mothers invention.
My hearing's assaulted by skittering paws
in the soffit above my computer,
caws rasp, dangerous dark wings thrum
at the sashes of bedroom windows,
hoarded acorns roll down drain pipes
and pile up in corners of the dark,
damp lower room where I store potatoes.
I give in, book a room at the Super 8,
and make plans to Amtrak south for the holidays.

--Pat Murphy McClelland

CHICAGO

My molecules vibrate to the readings: 42^0 North, 87^0 West.
"Welcome to Chicago O'Hare International Airport," the voice booms
forth.
This is much more – this is home.

The solid, Midwestern, brick bungalows with roots and loam,
a graph paper mapping of streets by day
and magical twinkling sodium vapor lamps by night.

Egalitarian sandy white beaches
lining the city's eastern perimeter,
a bus ride away from any home,
free to all.

A large city center of architectural gems stretching for miles,
fading down to ethnocentric neighborhoods
of sharply boundaried micro-nations.

I turn off the rental car GPS
and head north to my favorite hot dog stand.

This is home.

--Alice Meerson

2 GRAY HAIRS

I noticed 2 grey hairs
In the looking glass today
The sign of the times
Will not steal them away
It did lend a reminder
Of the hair of the dog
And the eye of the tiger
And of brushed-off brain fog
That a precious life is short
For my companion, my love
And only determined
By the Dog-God above
Those few sprigs of aging
Will hold me to heart
That one day my lover and I
Will part
So better to savor
And make a vow
To enjoy every gray hair
RIGHT NOW

--Jill Meunier

FALLING IN MONROVIA CANYON

I slipped and fell into the creek.
Cool, clear water leapt up to kiss me
as I collapsed into the shallow stream,
suddenly pressed in mud
as a flower finds
it has been pressed
into a book, or the book
finds the flower
pressed into its pages.

To be flung forward—
a headlong revelation,
to feel the earth's bed
against me, flat and finite,
river and I both held close
in fertile canyon walls,
the heedful canopy,
leaves chattering, cooing,
the woods, the words
humming, white alder,
oak and sycamore,
tenderhearted, antiseptic,
the runic smell of fresh print,
love and eucalyptus.

I am not unfamiliar with falling
in and out of poems, in and out
of spaces, in and out of favor,
falling from rocks, from curbs,
from stars, from grace.

Relocation is always
imminent. To fall
is to be startled
into life again,
to invoke another spell,
to be bound into another
latitude of wonder.

--Mary Monroe

SONG OF TSUNAMI

I.
Waiting for the bodies to wash up on shore,
snow lightly dazzling, survivors shutter-eyed
pick through the pieces. One small, tired dog
bares his valiant teeth, growls as if whispering,
guards the still body of another dog.

II.
It mattered how fast you could run,
who was and was not claimed,
the world forced forward,
the wave crying, babies crying,
talking heads talking. *The resilient people
will rebuild.* But water was only
the beginning, radiation laughing.
No one could stop what would never
be over. Not even hope survives
what people do.

III.
They say the birds stopped
singing, waiting for the bodies
to wash up on shore.

IV.
The starfish began to melt
and then disappeared.
The butterfly's two left wings fused together.
The frog's skin is so clear you can see his organs
through his torso, with unfinished lumps
where his legs should be.

IV.
The soft brown deer stares at me,
confused, with her six legs,
two in front, four in back,
turns to an awkward gallop,
like a drunken spider
in the withered grass.

--Mary Monroe

MY BETTY*

Darling! I have stood in amazement gazing at autumn
trees painted by winter's magic brush,

Seeing reflections of frost-born colors in frozen ponds nestled
among majestic, snow-laced mountains.

I have cruised on serene, moonlit seas and watched silver fish
fly by the ship's radiant, phosphorous bow.

I have watched the first piercing rays of dawn silhouette
a cloudless horizon.

These views I have seen from the deck of a trim, mighty fighting
ship—describable, inspiring beauty.

When you embrace me, I see deep in your eyes a beauty
indescribable, a beauty that flows like a river,

Such that words cannot describe it. Musicians cannot orchestrate it.
Artists cannot paint it.

--Franklin D. Murdock

* First published in a prior version in the author's book, *My Life in Poetry and The Absolute Truth* (XLibris, 2002).

MANY MANSIONS

Each house you live in lives in you.
It doesn't matter that others' lives
have flowed through them and will flow through.
They are mapped in a surreal, so-real tangle
of dorms, apartments, foreign scenes
and grandparents' houses just around corners.
Drive by one of these, pull over.
Look past the lawn to the front door.
The house before you barely exists
compared to the one living in you.

We went back by a tiny house
next to a gas station at a bus stop.
In our living room, Nyal's Barber Shop
with a swiveling red leather chair.
Under the ceiling, a model train
ran around the room on a ledge.
We didn't need haircuts—
Nyal let us go back to see our bedroom,
where dogs were groomed.
No dream except the American one!

That's not the way it usually is.
Present occupants are mysterious.
You drive off hoping they didn't notice,
leave to them the laughter, plumbing, carpet,
the blowing fuses, the messy tree.
The house, in the meantime, drives off in you.

Old Mr. Vodka improving *The Wasteland*
when read aloud. The couch turquoise vinyl,
the rag rug green-blue. No barber chair.
You can so easily take yourself there.

--Janet Nippell

PINK PEARL ERASER

The third grade girl, the homework sheet,
three paragraphs that tell
of multiplying and dividing as reciprocal.
They are opposites, she writes, to answer question one.
Four more questions follow, detailed yet vague.
OK, I say, *let's read again. What are they looking for?*
and even for me, reading, it begins to blur —
math tricks you'd show on a board overgrown with words.

But on each line, each runway, she lands her pencil, clear:
So I can get the anser right. Use one to check the other.
She's eight years old! They ask, How will all this
help you when you get to higher math?
So I can get the anser right in algebra, she writes.

I give up misguiding her toward mirroring that text.
I hope her teacher will agree she has grasped the gist.

Her pencil point's reciprocal rubbed to its ring of tin,
I pull out my Pink Pearl. I tell her that her *anser*
needs a *w* within. One of those funny spellings
in English, I explain. (That *w* a witness, zigzag DNA
carrying *andswaru*, a rebuttal sworn to.)

The Pink Pearl is slanted, with an edge that leads the way.
It bends and wiggles softly as she undoes each wrong place
and in the clearing carefully fits a penciled *wer*.
She hands the Pink Pearl back to me — reciprocal, from her.

--Janet Nippell

118

THE HAIRDRESSER'S WIFE

I would rather die
now with nothing
spoiled still.
Leave you with
untarnished dreams
all sweetness
intact.

What's best? The
past happiness
nobody can steal
or the happiness
you presently
own that could be
ripped away?

What is best?
What bloomed
was harvested
stocked in memory
or what's here but
might perish fade
disappear?

I would like to die
now leave you
with this miracle
I didn't create
and I guess I
can't grant.

Rather
vanish
be nothing but what
you'll remember
my name
in your mouth
my place
in your heart.

--Toti O'Brien

LIKE A GOURD, WITH DRIED SEEDS THAT RATTLE

My womb is hollow.
It is where my dreams sleep
Nestled inside of me, resting against the fleshy sides of my uterus,
Nursed by my blood,
Sharing my oxygen,
Taking nourishment from my nourishment,
Which is sometimes food, and sometimes verse.

They are hidden in the hollow of what makes me feminine,
Of what has and will continue to
Define me.

They are out of reach.
No prying hands or questions can touch them as they
Rest against the parts I cannot share.

My womb is like a gourd with dried seeds that rattle,
And tell the story of things withered and dead,
Trapped within the walls that created them.

--Sharaya Olmeda

TRESPASSSER

Oxy Acetylene Welding Machine,
You daunting, masculine brute.
When I lift your wand, its weight feels comfortably cumbersome,
Like an appendage I was born without.

The hiss in your hose is an insecure man's disapproval.
I am the snake of corruption.
I wear red lipstick.

My femininity is a slap in the face to the cherished idea of
The virile workshop.
The tits and ass talk.
The finger through a circle
Motion.

The mask sinks slowly over my brow,
Lubricated by my sweat,
Which is as salty and stinging as
The sweat the men around me
Are damp with.

The spark lighter makes a finger snap sound,
An attention-getting,
Beckoning-the-waitress
Sound.

A flash of white-hot flame rimmed orange and blue,
Erupts from the tip like suppressed opinions.
It is wild
And powerful
And feminine.

White-hot sparks fly around my helmet like insults.
I bathe in their cathartic rain
And emerge a feminist forged in the fires of
A fickle
Double
Standard.

--Sharaya Olmeda

DISCLAIMER

I've grown tired of staring
at the top of your head,
counting the soon-to-be grays.
Look up from your device
and stare into my eyes,
admire them, fall into them.
Surprise me one morning
and call them brunet
instead of dark brown.

Forget the Bronx accent slipping out
after a second glass of
wine, gin, or vodka

and the way it prevents me
from pronouncing words correctly, like
Paul, coffee, off, or long.

Stop checking me in
and taking a picture of
every flower or epicurean delight.
I'd rather taste the day
off our skins,
savoring with each tongue stroke.
Hug my mofongo loving
chichos and ask me if
I want seconds.
Slip your hands around my muffin top
and guide us into a slow dance

with the hums of your mouth.
Fill me up like a teacup
with promises of unplugging
and breathing in the present,

where my eyes
are the only thing
illuminating your face.

--Luivette Resto

LIKE MOTHER, LIKE DAUGHTER

The blend of Newports
and wine on my breath
remind me of her
as I light my next cigarette.

Holding it the way she does,
poised and lady-like
when she holds court during
unsanctioned smoke breaks.

Curve my left eyebrow like her
when I hear bullshit pick-up lines
or excuses masked as reasons,
talk with my hands
as I spew Spanish curses at
NASCAR-worthy speed.
We hold our vulnerabilities
like we hold back our tears,
with purpose and protectiveness.

Smile when we really want
the earth to swallow us whole,
enjoy the silence of solitude
(a bit too much perhaps),

dream to be a starfish
because, like comic book heroes,
they possess regenerative super powers.
Like the intersections of a Venn Diagram,

we share the shame of early pregnancies,
disgust for tolerated slaps to the face, but
today I rewrite the plot of our lives,
flicking ashes on the ground,
knowing we will be them one day.

--Luivette Resto

ODE TO MENUDO

Not the slang term for money,
the Spanish translation for *often*,
or the traditional Sunday morning
Mexican hangover cure.

Ode to the Puerto Rican Menudo:
Renee, Johnny, Xavier, Miguel, and Ricky,
(before Martín).
The original Latin boy band,
gracing record covers
with feathered hair and curly mullets,
skin tight, blindly bright
primary-colored pleathered pants,
satin shirts with plunging necklines,
showing off a pectoral landscape
of early pubescent chest hair stubble.

I was part of Menudomania.
Wore my I heart Menudo t-shirt and side ponytail
as I waited in line to watch their movie,
Una Aventura Llamada Menudo,
in a claustrophobic new city called The Bronx.

I was home for eighty-three minutes,
listening to my native tongue on the silver screen,
with its inflections, intonations,
and sing-song melodies.
Eighty-three minutes of forgetting why I had to leave

my classmates, cousins, and the sunrises
off the mountainside of Aguas Buenas.
Sang along to "A Volar," wishing I could hop
on an air balloon ride back to the familiar.

--Luivette Resto

BIRD HAND

always been this way, she
says, with sparrows and others
gliding through open windows,
alighting on her
hand, their
feathers weightless

she beads slivers of
last night's bread,
feeds crushed grains
on fingertips
to wisp-beaks,
palm tickled by twig feet,
brushed by wingtips
of these visitors from
clouds and trees

their wings, her hand,
all one: touches of dew,
kisses of breeze,
sunlight dipped with mist

big-boned girl, kneecaps
huge from mops and
pails, eyes heavy
counting cents,
arms lead weights
at dusk

but she soars with birds
in hand,
kindred spirits, lilting
on currents gold,
morning birds
in peace and shade,
cool slants of dawn,
transparent bones,
everything
lightened
of
earth

--Thelma T. Reyna

TILL THE VERY END

*"98-Year-Old Vet Dresses in Uniform One Last Time
On Veteran's Day, Dies Hours Later"*
-- Huffington Post, November 2014

Master Sergeant Justus straightens
his lapels at noon, salutes the nurse,
and rests against his weary pillow.

Colors swim in Master Sergeant dreams—
blue of smoke, white of bone, red of
sundered limbs.

His leathered palms still curl
around grenades or comrades' hands
in blasted fields.

His fingers still shove bayonets
in rifle mouths, brave legs churning
past machine gun spit.

Time is hard when death is all a hero
has, despite parades, trumpets, and
medals arrayed on chests.

Master Sergeant lies eyes-closed at
dusk, gloves pristine, dress blues spiffed,
eternally pressed.

--Thelma T. Reyna

GOD IS IN THE WAVES*

He told you once God is under water.
Said to everyone, "Why worry? Let's go
sailing." You who were not wife nor daughter
but friend, who loved him, hoped this to be so,
that in the final dive, he would lose grief,
find peace in mackerel, tuna, coral reef.

I see you at the edge of frothing sea,
looking for a sign amidst stone and wood.
I wish I could tell you with certainty
angels consoled him. The truth is I could

not know. I do know God is the design
present in this storm, and in these great waves
takes us sailing in purifying brine,
brings us back beyond the water, earth, graves.

--Susan Rogers

*Originally published in a prior version in the anthology, *Woman in Metaphor 2013*, edited by Maria Elena B. Mahler.

SAVING FLOWERS: A TANKA PROSE

Once a month I arrange flowers at the regional headquarters of Sukyo Mahikari. Last Sunday, I did my best to use flowers that were asking to be displayed: three wide-faced sunflowers, elegant birds of paradise, orange petals fanned—and several stalks of irises, purple-tipped with color so deep, I wanted to drink their ink like wine. No room for the beautiful lily, so I cut its stem and placed it where it could be used another day. Then I took care to gather all the fallen blooms, the "filler" stems and shortest flowers that could not be placed in a giant vase and took them home with me. On my way out I chanced to look at the shelf for shoes. There, lying across a shelf so low I needed to kneel to reach them, were forgotten flowers—violet gladioli and long-stemmed daisies, almost gone. Perhaps someone left them there thinking to take them home. I felt their waste in my heart. Not wanting to accept their loss, I lifted each gently as I would a hurt bird and brought them to the entryway. Using scissors, I cut them, surgically, trying to give each a chance to survive. Then I placed them one by one in a vase to greet visitors by the door.

Spring Ceremony
in the silence
of the golden shrine
surrounded by purifying snow
I offer apology

--Susan Rogers

NEOCON BLUE

Green how I want you green.
Green wind. Green branches.
The ship on the sea
And the horse on the mountain.
        --Garcia Lorca, *Havard*

Blue I don't want you.
Blue curses, blue truths,
storms on the blue lake
cast waves to the sky.
The lifeguard slides down
the snowy mountains
to the delta.
Hidden in the white
snow drifts, depressed
philosophers slide with
heads upside down.

Blue how I hate you blue.
Floating along the Potomac
boatloads of metallic
etchings portraying children
swept from school yards,
barriers across
hospitals, blue nuns,
blown up chimneys,
blue Pin stripes flown in on brooms.

I was like you Mr. Blue.
In freshman summer,

I cuddled with Iron Ayn's
novels, but now
bloated Mooches
swim up pool ladders
from sewers
to high Washington
verandas.

A blue flag swirling in
red flames, exploding
stars and cocaine bars.
Above the prison catwalk,
blue blouses stained
in scarlet varnish.
Neon eyelids
stuffed in blue hoods
scan the yellow streets
of the neighborhoods.

The statue of Liberty
goes for a swim.
In the ballroom,
the blind accountant
dispenses eviction notices.

--Ed Rosenthal

*Originally published in "Beyond the Lyric Moment" (Tebot Bach Publishers, 2014).

ROSE OF TRANSIT

Climbing icy steps to the el train
is my mother.
Rose of slushy sidewalk treks
from stations to city office.

She is a songbird romancing
astonished strangers
at crowded delis.

She is a long phone call
with the wrong person
then wild laughter.

She is smiling at me
in a white lace gown
in a white frame
forever.

She is a polio-stricken woman
with arms slicing the waves
of blue ocean.

Rose! I see you throw your
crutches on the seashore
with abandon.

You are the one

of shining Iron.
I'm not the son
of a man.

--Ed Rosenthal

A PANTOUM

This morning was dark
Two can live as cheaply as one
Somewhere there are dragons
Is that all there is?

Two can live as cheaply as one
At least that is what they say
Is that all there is?
There is more, really

At least that is what they say
Who is "they"?
There is more, really
We just have to uncover it

Who is "they"?
They may lurk in the darkness
We just have to uncover it
And avoid the dragons

They may lurk in the darkness
They wait for the light
And avoid the dragons
While they constantly search for the truth

They wait for the light
They look for the light at the end of tunnels
While they constantly search for the truth
And once finding it, they rejoice

They look for the light at the end of tunnels
It's there, though hard to find sometimes
And once finding it, they rejoice.
Their quest is fruitful.

--Elsa M. J. Seifert

THERE WAS SOMETHING THAT I ASKED OF YOU

But you forgot it. I wanted you to call me.
You tell me that I mean more to you
than anything else in the world.
And yet you forget to call me.

We've traveled to Hawai'i,
hiked the mountains, snorkeled and biked to the beach.
We cooked Moo Goo Gai Pan in the wok together for dinner.
Do you remember?

When I speak, am I a little noise, nothing more?
Pleasant, yes, but with no substance, no meaning for you?
When you do phone, you tell me you just want to hear my voice.
Do you really hear anything I say to you?

I ask myself, is it important that you hear me while you sit,
Wordless, deaf, in front of your TV screen?
I know what I say, and I know myself and the substance of my words,
but is it important that you know them, too?

--Elsa M. J. Seifert

TWISTED TREE

roots cracking the sidewalk
branches spread like outstretched arms
to make a playground for
the little boy climbing
falling
crying for his mother

how I long to hold him

--Nancy Shiffrin

FIVE MODERN REFLECTIONS ON BASHO'S ANCIENT POND

Furu ike ua
kawazu tobikomu
mizu no oto.

An ancient pond
A frog jumps in
The splash of water.
--Matsuo Bashō, 1644-1694

*　*　*　*

Ancient forest
blasted off mountaintop
for coal

Splash of fish
no longer heard in lake
water used for fracking

Frogs jump no more
in rainforest pond
one degree climate change—too hot

Silent Spring
of Rachel Carson
becoming acid ocean

Cowboys and Indians
fight Keystone Pipeline,
not each other

--Carl Stilwell

THANKING THE BIRDS

While Swift Eagle walks on reservation,
he hears sounds of boys playing in the bushes.
"There's another one. Shoot it!" shouts one boy.

He pushes through the bush and sees
a boy holding a BB gun while his buddies
stand around a dead chickadee, robin
and several blackbirds.

"Ah," he says, "I see you have been hunting.
Pick up your game and come with me."
He leads them to a ground where they can
build a fire and cook the birds.

Before they eat, Swift Eagle says, "It is important
to thank the birds for the gift of their songs,
feathers and bodies as food."

As they eat, he tells stories.
After his last story, he says, "You know the Great Spirit
gave the gift of life to everything that is alive.
Life is a very sacred thing.

"But our Creator knows we have to eat to live.
That is why it's permitted to hunt
to feed ourselves.

"So I understand you boys must have been
very, very hungry
to kill these little birds."

--Carl Stilwell

ROSE PARADE

A wet cigarette end
In the gutter off Colorado Blvd
Whispers memories of New Year's morning,
Sounds of so many people like the
Crackling of campfires, reunion late at night.

--James Storbakken

SAL'S PIZZERIA

Stretching up like wheat to touch the sky,
Bruises on my arms from plowing through
Hoards of Mr. He'll Do's,
My heart rose and bronzed
Like hot dough in the black air
Of the Upper East Side.

On the other side of the pane,
Ragged New Yorkers dragged themselves through gray,
But I felt light.

Somewhere between the marinara pools
And the mesh of mozzarella,
I lost myself in you.
And in speaking of your arms,
Old poets sat up in my mind and spoke,
For the first time in years.
They said, "Come live with me and be my love,
And we will some new pleasures prove."

Hours later, home, I knew
Such new shades of green inside.
That night, the ceiling cried.
And your kiss,
Soft, like the leather of a cat's ear
on my mouth,
Tasted new.

--AASullivan

ARGOSIES

I stood on the floor of the high school gymnasium.
I beheld the reunion that commenced
and remembered the nights of decades ago.

Adorned in jackets of maroon and white,
you made your way down boulevards of youthful
abandon and unfathomed adventure.
Your carnal red convertibles were your masted Argos.
Your companions gathered from home team victories
became your fellow Argonauts.
The guard rails and traffic lights were your Symplegades.

The blue boys with silver badges who sought
to quell your adolescent storms became your dragon-toothed armies.
Your fellow motorists competing for the downtown
strip transformed into perilous herds of centaurs.
The waitresses at Pal's Diner became your daughters of Pelias,
and the prom queen and her attendants were the royal Medeas who
kept you spellbound.

And now.....your once-sculpted torsos sag with the burden of years.
Your full-blown manes of hair are reduced to winsome strands.
Your athletic sprints devolve into slouches and saunters.
You've hung up your tapered oars and replaced them with briefcases.
The objectives of once-fabled quests are now the stuff of mortgages,
dividends, T-notes and your son's tuitions.

And your golden fleeces that were then more coveted than anything,
and hung tantalizing from tree branches guarded by fearsome
serpents: What of them?

The illusions of fulfillment, the empty promises of power, the
arrogance of riches
to which we've all succumbed at times in the ocean of journeys?
How often did they prove to be no more than that?

In the end the serpent saves us a seat on the mirrored shore of
judgment, and the Golden Fleece
is our tiny thread in the needle's eye of infinity.

--Brian John Thorpe

FOOTSTEPS AT DAWN

Morning embraces the city scape
with the sound of human feet meeting stone, turf or asphalt.
How they scurry, amble, run, halt or stroll!

Are mine among them?
Yes, but not of my choosing.
I'd rather dance in the astral lights, run wildly from planet
to star, from moon to moon, and, after pausing to behold with awe
the majesty of each, rest at last on sensual clouds, perch on
desert monuments, settle on snow-glistened mountains or nestle in
tropical trees.
I prefer the extravagant corridors of fervent dreams to the brick-lined
streets
of urban toil.

I defy time as well as space.
Dismissing the inexorable din of the
present, I choose to meander among visages of
myth with ancient seers, converse with Greeks beneath the shadows
of the Parthenon,
set forth with Caesars from the heart of the forum, regale with
Plantagenets,
brave the fates of the Dardanelles, inspire revolutions, quell the beast
of petty tyranny and champion the sanctity of art!
I claim all that is or has been, to mold, command and reshape as I
like, whatever its dimensions, dictates or destinies.

But then there is that startled moment.
The chill grey of daybreak seizes me again and
rudely places me in the hurried thrall of my urban fellows.

Shall I proceed with them, commence with the herd, lose myself in
their furious multitude?
Or shall I stand still, calm and pensive, awaiting the next gust of wind
to carry me aloft
in fevered flights of fantasy?

--Brian John Thorpe

UNDER THE CANOPY

Beneath a verdant canopy, I walk in late afternoon.
I look up to see the branches of a hundred trees enjoining.
The cool, resulting penumbra is soothing at first, but at last it defies
and obscures the light when I need it most within and without.

Too long have I embraced the shade. Too long have I succumbed and
been enticed by the songs of shadow.
I wish to be reborn beneath a splendid, and as yet unseen, firmament.
Poisonous potions, powders, and concoctions have for years dulled
my reason and
plunged my soul into a fitful sleep or deadening stupor.
As such, I have been like an inmate seeking flight from grey,
impervious stone
or unyielding iron bars.

Will the canopy allow it, or, as it has so many times in the past,
transform itself from a gracious arch into something akin to black
damask, or the deepening gray of some toxic miasma?
Will its branches convolute? Will its vines create a stranglehold and
the spare gaps between them form pairs of baleful eyes, conniving
smiles, or pitiless frowns?

As I move, will it unleash a knotting gnarl of twine as if to
herald a sudden nightfall that I may or may not want?
And if I don't, will it summon forth unnameable creatures that sleep
by day, only to stir
in hours void of sun and form a host of ominous watchers?

I have paid many debts to shade and darkness. I feel that I owe them
no more.

Hence, I implore whatever hand may control them, let the branches
reach upward to welcome a presence warm and golden, brimming
with the promise of splendid hues.
Let furies be gone and Euminides triumph!
Let the shroud of night and death be banished by Aurora's fearless
laughter.
Let the canopy of branch and twine open to infinite radiance,
and shower my meager path with blossoms rare, ripe with new faith,
candescent and alive!

--Brian John Thorpe

DIVINATOR

Burrows
straight
down
into
the soil,
wresting aside
stones,
cracking rocks,
pushing
through bony
apertures,
sunless pale
forager,
snaggletooth
looking for
its mate to
tap: root.

--Mary Torregrossa

WALKING YORKSHIRE

"I'll walk where my own nature will be leading."
--Emily Bronte

A wide expanse
of green mossy
mounds, a boggy
mess of land where
thick fog banks linger
long, where after drizzle,
mist ensues. And when
the day burns bright
and the robin's-egg
blue sky polishes our eyes,
we are reminded by old
Nellie Dean, warning while
we walk – not to be deceived.
Not to scurry nor to slip
but take a measured step,
though quick, and look
before you leap, as you might
land your boot in some hidden
glassy pool or maybe even
fall, head over heels,
into the marshy and uneven
moor.

--Mary Torregrossa

IMAGES EDGED IN BLUE WALLS

Time elapses as pyramid glyphs
deciphered into shattered
pieces of jade shade eyes.

At the even of midnight
bears traverse leagues.
Deer antlers cast shadows –light.

Gold beams of light
from sun showers brown eyes.
Read into the symmetry of flowers.

--Jose Trejo-Maya

IMAGES INCISED INTO HOLOGRAMS

New night shifts into kaleidoscope.
Edges of crescent moon,
stars align into frost dew.

Scribes reach back
to a time when stones bled
hieroglyphs in ideographic.

Hawks fly serpentine
at thirty degrees,
sun color invisible.

--Jose Trejo-Maya

A STUDY WITH CHERRIES*

After Etude in C Major, Op. 10, No. 1 and
a cherry orchard of my grandparents,
Maria Anna and Stanislaw Wajszczuk

I want a cherry,
a rich, sweet cherry
to sprinkle its dark notes
on my skin, like rainy preludes
drizzling through the air.
Followed by the echoes
of the piano, I climb
a cherry tree to find rest
between fragile branches
and relish the red perfection—
morning cherry music.
Satiated, sleepy,
I hide in the dusty attic.
I crack open the shell
of a walnut to peel
the bitter skin off,
revealing white flesh—
a study in C Major.
Tasted in reverie,
the harmonies seep
through light-filled cracks
between weathered beams
in Grandma's daily ritual
of Chopin at noon.

--Maja Trochimczyk

* From *Chopin with Cherries: A Tribute in Verse*, ed. by author (Moonrise Press, 2010).

THE SUMMER OF LOVE*

She would never be as beautiful again as she had been
that summer in Germany. Blue eyes shining
from under the tightly-tied kerchief,
blond curls shorn short for work.
They planted potatoes side by side in the fields.
He was tall, kind, athletic, son of the Bauer.
She blushed a pretty shade of pink
when she caught his eye.

It was their first love. They were so shy,
led side by side with jeering cardboard signs,
noisy blasts of trombones. A feast for the whole village.
Kids ran in circles around them, laughing –
The Polish Pig. The Traitor of our Race.
Bronia and Hans. People poked them,
pushed them, shaved their heads.
Identical, grotesque, bald puppets,
each with a single lock left hanging
in the middle of the forehead.

She was sent to Auschwitz.
He – to the eastern front.
It was their last summer.

--Maja Trochimczyk

*Originally published in the author's book, *Slicing the Bread* (Finishing Line Press, 2014).

WHAT ONCE WAS

I stop to chat with an elderly woman sitting in her driveway, with veined hands resting in her lap, white hair curled and lacquered. Waiting for her grandson to drive her to the hospital, she talks about the good old days. "I was 18 when I won the first prize in a dance competition at the Palladium. In my poodle skirt, I was flying through the air like a whirlwind." She falls silent, looks up from her wheelchair, far into the past. "I was too young to be allowed to go there. My Mom did not even know. I gave the trophy to someone else. I went out with my boyfriend, whom I later married. We were together for 43 years." Her smile brightens, then curls on her lips, as she adds: "When I was 30, my husband said, 'Aren't you too old to dance like that?' I answered: 'You are never too old to dance the jitterbug.'"

> loud music opens
> a bouquet of twirling skirts –
> dancing nights

--Maja Trochimczyk

BELL LETTERS: PARODY OF NURSERY RHYME, "BELLS OF LONDON"

"Oranges and lemons"
sings Samuel Langhorne Clemens
"Henchmen and Hitmen"
sings Good Gray
poet Walt Whitman
.

"Heaven and Hell-ville"
whales Herman Melville
"Drunk to a stupor"
sings James Fennimore Cooper

"Guns across
the Sea of Azov"
sings Good Doctor
Isaac Asimov.

--Jonathan Vos Post

BEAUTIFUL MUM*

enhanced with lavender
around edges of petals
frames a deep purple
spot that makes
blossoms stand out
amongst dark-colored
chrysanthemums

at your loveliness
my heart fills with joy
my depression
vanishes

you uplift
me and
bless someone else's
day with hope

--Lori Wall-Holloway

* Originally published in a prior version in *San Gabriel Valley Poetry Quarterly*, Issue 65, Spring 2015.

MIDNIGHT SHIFT

I quietly observe
desert life unfold
in the darkness
while I sit on my watch

Hidden by night
outlines of rabbits
come alive and venture
forth for food and play
amongst Joshua Trees

I sense other animals
join them until
starlight betrays
their cover to hungry
predators

As daylight gradually
emerges, the lively
creatures scamper off.
My shift is over.

--Lori Wall-Holloway

NEW SEASON OF HOPE*

As darkness
of the past fades
into what will
never be lived again,
a light bursts forth
on the horizon
of the present
to shine on
the future,
a fresh road
leading to days
unlike those
ever lived before

Here a new hope
springs up
that is open
to Father God
longing
to encircle
us with love
as a parent
who nurtures
and cares for a child

--Lori Wall-Holloway

* Originally published in a prior version in *2014 San Gabriel Valley Poetry Calendar*.

HAIR GLORIOUS

big bountiful full fluffy hair
it forms upon my head like a puff of glory
bouncing to the rhythm of my stride
defying gravity

wavy crinkles of midnight beauty
take a timely lift and fall
taunted and teased by the wind
swinging vivaciously

tightly curled spiral patterns
closely cloaking the curvaceous head
a sculptured magnificence
holding onto the testimonials of ancient times

straight loose fly-away strands
taking flight in whispered softness
seductively swinging to and fro
as the ocean pendulates ebbs and flows

--Jacquelyn Bellard Wilson

AUTHOR BIOGRAPHIES

RICARDO LIRA ACUÑA
Acuña was born and raised on the U.S./Mexico border in Nogales, AZ, and earned his BA degree from Stanford University in English and French Literatures; and his MFA in Screenwriting from Columbia University. Acuña has published two books of poetry and photography: *Greetings from Heaven & Hell*; and *under the influence*. He has also written and produced the PBS-award-winning short film, *L.A. Noir*; published a graphic novel, *The Realm*; and is currently working on the publication of his first novel, *Prodigal Son*.

PETROUCHKA ALEXIEVA
Alexieva is well-known as a feminist, a LOVE poet, writer and distinguished scholar. She was published at age 16 in the national poetry magazine *Rodna Rech* in Bulgaria. She graduated *Cum Laude* from the California State University, Los Angeles, and received an "All-American Scholar Award." She has performed her works in Australia, Hungary, Romania, Transylvania, Bulgaria, and nationwide in the US. Her work appears in anthologies, feminist magazines, and newspapers.

KHADIJA ANDERSON
Pushcart Prize-nominated poet, Butoh dancer, and Muslim convert, Khadija Anderson has had over 50 poems published in print and online. She holds an MFA in Creative Writing from Antioch University in Los Angeles. Her first book of poetry, *History of Butoh,* was published in 2012 by Writ Large Press. Find her at www.khadijaanderson.com .

VIBIANA APARICIO-CHAMBERLIN
Aparicio-Chamberlin recently performed her poetry and bilingual stories at the Pasadena History Museum, the Vincent Price Museum, Rock Rose Art Gallery, Beyond Baroque, and Vroman's Book Store. Her Chicano memoirs are published by the Pasadena Weekly, and presented by Brooklyn and Boyle Magazine. Bambaz Press will publish her book, *Mi Amor: Stories of Family Love*, in 2015.

MARIA A. ARANA
Maria A. Arana is a teacher, writer, and poet. Learn more about her at www.rainingvoices.blogspot.com

MARCIA ARRIETA

Marcia Arrieta is a poet, artist, and teacher. Her work appears widely in the small press. She is the author of one poetry book, *triskelion, tiger moth, tangram, thyme* (Otoliths); and two chapbooks, *experimental: (Potes & Poets)* and *the curve against the linear* (Toadlily Press Quartet Series—*An Uncommon Accord*). Through the years, Arrieta has led various writing workshops throughout greater Los Angeles. She edits/publishes *Indefinite Space*.

BETH BAIRD

Beth Baird enjoys spoken word, theater, and music. She has written more than 30 songs which were performed by her former band, Modern Society. Baird loves to write comedic pieces as well as serious works and recently read a collection of her work for the Arroyo Channel Show, "Spending a Little Time with Poetry." She now reads her work internationally, most recently in Norway. Baird is married to William Davis. They have three children and live in Altadena, CA.

TIM CALLAHAN

Callahan is an artist who worked for many years in the animation industry. He had written some poetry since he was in his thirties but didn't write in earnest until he was in his middle sixties. A published author, he regularly contributes articles to *Skeptic Magazine*. He lives with his wife, Bonnie, in the foothills of Altadena on the edge of the Angeles National Forest and often hikes the Sunset Ridge Trail. Callahan served on this anthology's Selection Committee.

DON KINGFISHER CAMPBELL

A multi-award-winning poet listed on the *Poets and Writers* website, Campbell has been a coach/judge for Poetry Out Loud; a performing poet/teacher for Red Hen Press Youth Writing Workshops; Los Angeles Area Coordinator and Board Member of California Poets in the Schools; publisher of the *San Gabriel Valley Poetry Quarterly*; leader of the Emerging Urban Poets Writing and Deep Critique workshops; and various other prominent Southern California poetry programs. For publication credits, see www.dkc1031.blogspot.com

GLORIANA CASEY

Gloriana Casey has been a teacher, a business writer for a weekly, a copywriter and arts reviewer for a Midwestern TV station, a dinner theatre actress, and a SAG/AFTRA member. Along the way, she even learned to milk a cow by hand.

She loves rhyming and acrostics in her poetry. Casey served on this anthology's Selection Committee.

VICTOR CASS

Cass has a BFA with Honors from Art Center College of Design in Pasadena, and an MA from American Military University, in Manassas Park, VA. He is the author of several books, both fiction and nonfiction. His short stories, articles, and essays have appeared in *Arroyo Monthly Magazine, Pasadena Weekly, Pasadena Star-News, If & When Literary Journal, Mexican War Journal,* and other publications.

JACKIE CHOU

Chou holds a BA degree in Creative Writing from the University of Southern California. Since childhood, she used writing as a tool to cope with a chaotic family and an overbearing mother, starting by writing diaries. Chou has been writing poetry since high school.

MICHELLE CHUNG

Chung grew up in Seoul, Korea. She made her poetry debut with the Hanmak Literature Emerging Poet Award (1997) for her literary criticism from "Literature and Consciousness" in Korea (2010). Chung also received the 14th Kasan Literary Award for her poetry in the US (2008). She is currently editor-in-chief of *Global Poetry & Poetics, Mijusihak,* from the Korean Poets Society of America. She has published two books of poetry, including *Reveries of the Street* (2009), and has also been published in numerous anthologies.

STEPHEN COLLEY

Colley is a retired software engineer who has resided in Altadena for 22 years. He has written and performed classical music, including soprano and piano settings of 15 Robert Frost. Colley has also written three screenplays and is a practicing poetaster.

BEVERLY COLLINS

Originally from New Jersey, Collins is the author of the book *Quiet Observations* and is one of three 2012 prize winners in a California State Poetry Society competition. Her work has appeared in *Poetry Speaks! Year of Great Poems and Poets Calendar; Bits & Pieces* magazine; *California Quarterly; San Gabriel Valley Poetry Quarterly; Patch.com; Poetry Letter and Literary Review,* among other publications.

YAGO S. CURA
An English teacher, Cura is the author of *Rubberroom* (2009) and co-author of *Odas a Futbolistas* (2010). His poetry has appeared in numerous literary journals, such as *Kweli, La Fovea, PALABRA, Borderlands,* and the *U.S. Latino Review*. His book reviews have appeared in *The St. Mark's Poetry Project Newsletter,* and *Hinchas de Poesia*. He is co-founder of the Copa Poetica, a three-day reading series in Los Angeles regarding the World Cup. His Spanglish blog, *Spicaresque*, has had more than 52,000 visitors.

PAULI DUTTON
Pauli Dutton, an award-winning poet who has been published in a number of anthologies, is active in several writing groups, including Poets on Site and the Emerging Urban Poets. Recently retired from Altadena Library District after almost 30 years, Pauli is now spending time with family and friends, singing, dancing, writing, and napping, her favorite way to write. She helped select poems for this anthology and was a consistent, valuable source of support.

RICHARD HAWKINS DUTTON
Dutton is married to Pauli Dutton, is retired from engineering and education, has three post-graduate degrees, some technical writing, and has published in four different poetry anthologies. Poetry has been his hobby for 10 years.

LYNN FAYNE
Fayne was born in California, graduated from UCLA with a BA, and graduated from San Fernando Valley College of Law with a JD degree. She is currently retired, writing occasionally and painting.

MARK A. FISHER
A writer, poet, and playwright living in Tehachapi, CA, his column, "Lost in the Stars," has appeared in Tehachapi's *The Loop* newspaper for several years. His plays have appeared on stages in Pine Mountain Club, Tehachapi, and Hayward. Fisher's poetry has been published in *A Sharp Piece of Awesome*, the *San Gabriel Valley Poetry Quarterly*, and *Gutters and Alleyways*.

MARTINA ROBLES GALLEGOS
Gallegos immigrated from Mexico as a teenager. She graduated from Pasadena High School and from California State University, Northridge, with a BA; enrolled in the Teacher Credential Program; and earned a degree in Bilingual Education. Gallegos worked for Hueneme Elementary School

District for almost 18 years. She suffered a massive stroke, heart surgeries, and other medical crises but is now working on a Master's degree. Gallegos has completed a full-length poetry book scheduled for publication in 2015-2016.

MIRIAM QUEZADA HAGERMAN

Hagerman is a retired elementary and high school teacher who has taught in the United States and Mexico City. She now works as a translator and lecturer. Her love of Mexican art and literature motivated her to write poetry and create folk art pieces from found objects. She has also conducted research on *rebozos* (traditional Mexican shawls) and historical Mexican literature. Hagerman has lectured at various prestigious galleries and libraries in the US and is currently working on writing her first children's book.

HAZEL CLAYTON HARRISON

A long-time resident of Altadena, Harrison is the author of *The Story of Christmas Tree Lane* and *Winter in L.A.* Her memoir, *Crossing the River Ohio*, was published in 2014. Her poetry has been published in *Conversations with Love, Poetically Speaking,* and other anthologies. Read more of her writings in her blog, www.hazelpearls.blogspot.com.

JOAN HOFFMAN

Hoffman is a partner and Director of Business Development and Strategic Planning for Fred Hoffman Architecture. She received a "Women Who Mean Business Award" from the *San Fernando Business Journal*. In addition to substantial civic involvements and leadership, she is a Performer/Writer at Free Clinic Sunset. Hoffman also hosted "A Woman's Point of View" on the COX cable network.

GERDA GOVINE ITUARTE

Ituarte's first poetry art book, *Oh Where is My Candle Hat?* (2012) was published in English and Spanish with a testimonial by Nikki Giovanni. Her second book, *Alterations | Thread Light Through Eye of Storm,* will be published in Spring 2015. Her poetry has appeared in the *San Gabriel Valley Poetry Quarterly, Poetry and Cookies, HomeTown Pasadena*, and *Frontera Esquina* magazine in Tijuana, B.C., Mexico. She has read her work widely, and helped select poems for this anthology. Her website is www.poetryartbookstation.com.

BRIONY JAMES

A graduate of Ithaca College with a dual degree in English and Theatre, Briony James transplanted from New York four decades ago and has found a place to bloom in Altadena. She wrote her first poem at age four and has not stopped. She has been published in *2014 Poetry and Cookies*, the *San Gabriel Poetry Quarterly*, SGVP *Calendar*, *Bright Stars* (Vols. 6 & 7), and *Ribbons*. Her work will appear in *Undertow Tanka Review*, Vol. 4, this winter.

LOIS P. JONES

Jones' poetry has appeared in publications such as *Narrative Magazine, American Poetry Journal, Tupelo Quarterly*, and *The Nassau Review*. *New Yorker* selected her poem "Ouija" as Poem of the Year in a 2010 competition. Jones won the 2012 Tiferet Poetry Prize and the 2012 Liakoura Prize. She is a host of "Poet's Café" (KPFK, Los Angeles 90.7 fm), and co-produces the Moonday Poetry Reading Series at Flintridge Books in La Canada, CA. She is Poetry Editor of *Kyoto Journal* and a multiple Pushcart Prize nominee.

lalo kikiriki

lalo kikiriki grew up in Texas and, after 10 years on Pacifica Radio Houston, moved to Los Angeles. Author of *Old Movies/Other Visions* (with Pamela Lynn Palmer, 1979) and *New Stuff* (1981, revised 1993), kikiriki earned a Master's Degree in Humanities from California State University, Dominguez Hills. Her poetry has appeared in publications such as *San Gabriel Valley Poetry Quarterly, Poetry and Cookies, Of the People, ZZyZx, Sunrunner, Peralta Press, Lummox, Poetic Diversity*, and the *Revolutionary Poets Brigade Anthology*.

MINA KIRBY

Mina Kirby is a retired professor of mathematics who has published eight chapbooks as well as a full-length book of poetry, *Threads of My Life*. Kirby has performed as Featured Poet at a number of venues in Southern California and Maryland. She lives in Altadena, CA, with her family and pets.

DEBORAH P. KOLODJI

Kolodji moderates the Southern California Haiku Study Group, affiliated with the USC Pacific Asia Museum. She is the California Regional Coordinator for the Haiku Society of America and the former president of the Science Fiction Poetry Association. She has published over 800 poems.

NANCY LIND

Lind is a retired teacher of English literature, mother of three, grandmother of one little boy; recent transplant to California from New York with her husband, Russ LaValle; Creative Writing student; and aspiring poet.

JOE LUSNIA

Husband, father, worker, and writer, Lusnia has been published in the *Pasadena Weekly, Pasadena Community College's Inscape Anthology,* and *Poetry and Cookies.*

RADOMIR VOJTECH LUZA

Born in Vienna, Austria, Luza is the Poet Laureate of North Hollywood and a Pushcart Prize nominee. His 25 books include poems that have appeared in nearly 60 literary journals, anthologies, and websites. Luza has featured his poetry regularly across the country and organized and hosted over a dozen readings in places such as New York City, New Jersey, Ft. Walton Beach, FL, and Los Angeles. Luza co-organizes and hosts "Unbuckled: No Ho Poetry," the longest-running literary series in North Hollywood.

KARINEH MAHDESSIAN

karineh mahdessian: i write. i love. i right. i eat. i rite. i breathe.

SHAHÉ MANKERIAN

Mankerian's recent manuscript, *History of Forgetfulness,* has been a finalist at four prestigious competitions: the 2013 Crab Orchard Series in Poetry Open Competition; the 2103 Bibby First Book Competition; the Quercus Review Press, Fall Poetry Book Award 2013; and the 2014 White Pine Press Poetry Prize. He serves as Principal of St. Gregory Hovsepian School in Pasadena, CA; is co-director of the Los Angeles Writing Project; and received the L.A. Music Center's BRAVO Award, honoring educational excellence in the arts.

MIRA N. MATARIC, Ph.D.

Mataric has taught English, Russian, and Creative Writing and edited a literary magazine for 20 years, actively organizing workshops and public readings. Her work is translated into several languages in international anthologies. She has written 37 books published in two languages (poetry, short stories, novels, memoirs, and translations of noted American and European authors). She is also the recipient of more than 20 international awards.

PAT MURPHY MCCLELLAND

McClelland's poems appear in the *Feile-Festa Literary Journal, Atlas Poetica, Poetry and Cookies Anthology,* and a chapbook, *Turnings.* She has published several children's books and has taught creative writing workshops in Los

Angeles and "Writing for Healing" at the UC/San Francisco Comprehensive Cancer Center. She is currently revising a memoir, *The Masks of Grief*.

ALICE MEERSON
Born and raised in Chicago, Meerson received a BA from the University of Illinois at Chicago with a major in history. She lived overseas for several years before settling in the Altadena/Pasadena area, where she earned an MA in Human Development from Pacific Oaks College. She taught Special Education for many years in Glendale, CA prior to formally retiring and continuing to teach, take classes, write, and travel.

JILL MEUNIER
Jill Meunier is a career travel agent and lifelong aspiring poet. Her heart and soul and love for dogs are evident in her poetry.

MARY MONROE
Born on a farm in Minnesota, Monroe has spent her life as a journalist, writer, editor, and poet. Her poems—which explore love, loss and extraordinary, everyday experiences—have appeared in the *L.A. Times*, *Tiferet Journal*, *FRE&D*, *Bloodroot*, and *North Country*. She has studied with various renowned poets and lives with her husband and family pets in Eagle Rock, CA.

FRANKLIN D. MURDOCK
A World War II veteran and legally blind writer, Murdock has achieved much as an author in almost 95 years of life. He has published seven books, been a radio host, blogger, and a dedicated Biblical scholar. He has written poetry, memoir, and scholarly, inspirational nonfiction. His most recent books are *From Alpha to Omega: The Absolute Truth* (2014) and *The Best Is Yet to Come* (2013). Murdock resides in Monrovia, CA, where he studies the Bible daily and continues to write and publish.**

JANET NIPPELL
Nippell was born and raised in Los Angeles and has lived in Pasadena since 1980. She has published in *Rattle*, *A Narrow Fellow*, and has a poem forthcoming in *Miramar*. She co-authored *Mostly on Foot: A Year in L.A.* (Floating Island, 1989), which narrates long walks in two voices.

TOTI O'BRIEN
O'Brien's poetry has been published in *Womb*, *Red Ochre*, *Black & White*, *If & When*, *Literary Mama*, and *Poetry Diversity*, among other journals. She has

published two children's books, two short story collections, and an essays miscellany in Italian. She has contributed to Italian magazines, such as *Mezzocielo, Salpare, L'Ostile,* and *Inguine.* She shares her backyard with a flock of roaming peacocks in the Los Angeles area.

SHARAYA OLMEDA

Olmeda has had a love affair with the written word since she was very young. She is currently a senior at California State University, Northridge, where she has earned a place on the Dean's List while studying for her Bachelor's degree in Creative Writing. In her free time, she enjoys thrift-shopping, visiting breweries, and playing board games with friends.

LUIVETTE RESTO

Resto was born in Aguas Buenas, Puerto Rico, but was raised in the Bronx. Her first book of poetry, *Unfinished Portrait,* was published in 2008 by Tia Chucha Press and was a Finalist for the 2009 Paterson Poetry Prize. She is a contributing poetry editor for *Kweli Journal;* a CantoMundo fellow; and a member of the advisory board of Con Tinta. Her book, *Ascension* (2013) was selected for the 2014 Paterson Award for Literary Excellence, awarded to previous Finalists of the Paterson Poetry Prize for continuing achievement.

THELMA T. REYNA

Thelma T. Reyna is the multiple-national award-winning author of four books: a short story collection (*The Heavens Weep for Us and Other Stories*), two poetry chapbooks (*Breath & Bone;* and *Hearts in Common);* and a full-length collection of her poems: *Rising, Falling, All of Us.* Her work has appeared in literary journals, anthologies, textbooks, blogs, and regional media off and on for over 30 years. She is Poet Laureate of the Altadena Library District, 2014-2016, and is editor of this anthology. She received a Ph.D. from UCLA.

SUSAN ROGERS

Rogers is a practitioner of Sukyo Mahikari— a practice promoting positive lifestyles (www.sukyomahikari.org). Read her in *Meditations on Divine Names: Woman in Metaphor,* as well as in various collections, including *San Diego Annual: The Best Poems of San Diego.* Her poetry was part of audio tours for the Pacific Asia Museum in Pasadena. Lois P. Jones' interview of her on KPFK's "Poets Café" is archived at www.timothy-green.org/blog/susan-rogers/

ED ROSENTHAL

Rosenthal is the former "Poet/Broker" of Downtown Los Angeles, who documented and criticized downtown development over 20 years, with his critiques published in the *LA Times, Wall Street Journal*, and other print media. He also read poetry publicly, depicting developers as cacti. He survived a near-death experience in the desert in 2010, which inspired his poetry book, *The Desert Hat*, published by Moonrise Press in 2013.

ELSA M. J. SEIFERT

A member of this anthology's Selection Committee, Seifert is a certified "Spiritual Director" and resident of Altadena for over 30 years. She studied at Immaculate Heart College and California State University, Los Angeles. She has worked as an editor and business manager; has had leadership roles in various organizations; and volunteers with Pasadena's homeless women and various interfaith groups. An author of poetry and short essays, she has been published in "The Courage to Write" and various anthologies.

NANCY SHIFFRIN

Nancy Shiffrin is the author of two collections of poetry, *The Vast Unknowing* (Infinity Publishing) and *Game with Variations* (unibook.com). Her reviews have appeared most recently in www.poetix.net and *The Lummox Journal*. Visit her at www.home.earthlink.net/~nshiffrin and www.nshiffrin@earthlink.net

CARL STILWELL

A retired teacher of Los Angeles City Schools, Stillwell's poetry has been published in *Blue Collar Review, Canary, Lummox, Poetry.com, Pearl, Prism, Revolutionary Poets Brigade--Los Angeles, San Gabriel Valley Poetry Quarterly*, and *Struggle*. His poems are also included in the anthologies, *An Eye for An Eye Makes the Whole World Blind: Poets On 9/11*; the annual anthology *Poetry and Cookies*; and *In the Arms of Words: Poems for Tsunami Relief.*

JAMES STORBAKKEN

Storbakken began writing poetry during his first year in college. Inspired by Jack Kerouac's *Dharma Bums*, Storbakken dropped out of college to hitchhike the Southwest and "roam Los Angeles streets at twilight." He enjoys singing the blues and reading.

AASULLIVAN

AASullivan has an MFA in Screenwriting and Poetry from Emerson College in Boston, Massachusetts. She is published as a poet, short story writer, and essayist. She is also an award-winning screenwriter and teleplay writer.

BRIAN JOHN THORPE

Thorpe is a poet, playwright, journalist, editor, critic, and actor. His work has appeared in publications as diverse as *The Hollywood Reporter, Cinefantastique Magazine,* and *San Gabriel Valley Poetry Quarterly.* Thorpe has served as assistant arts editor for the *Sun Reporter* in San Francisco; co-editor and co-publisher of the *West Coast Forum*; a member of the Synthaxis Theatre Co.; and a regularly featured poet at a number of local venues. He also lectures, tutors, and served on this anthology's Selection Committee.

MARY TORREGROSSA

An ESL teacher in the San Gabriel Valley (SGV), Torregrossa has facilitated poetry workshops for children, youth, and adults for the SGV Poetry Festival, organized special poetry events, and performed for charity fundraisers. She was selected as a 2009 "Newer Poet of LA" by the Los Angeles Poetry Festival. She has been featured in local media as well as published in literary journals and anthologies. She won the Whittier Writers Club Poetry Prize 2013, and the Poetry in the Windows 2014 award from the Arroyo Arts Collective.

JOSE TREJO-MAYA

Originally from the small pueblo of Tarimoro in Mexico, Trejo-Maya migrated to the US in 1988. His parents and grandparents had no formal education, but Trejo-Maya has earned three university degrees in the US, including an MFA in writing. His main academic interest is ethnopoetic language, with a particular interest in the ancient poet Netzahualcoyotl. Trejo-Maya's poems have been published in the *Nimrod International Poetry Journal, Belleville Park Pages, Star 82 Review, Visions International Review,* and *Lost Coast Review.*

MAJA TROCHIMCZYK, Ph.D.

A Polish-born poet, music historian, and photographer, Trochimczyk has published six books about music and five of poetry. Her poetry has appeared in anthologies and publications such as *The Loch Raven Review, Clockwise Cat, Epiphany Magazine, Lily Review, Ekphrasis Journal,* and *Quill and Parchment.* The Sixth Poet Laureate of Sunland-Tujunga, she is the founder of Moonrise Press, and Secretary of the Polish American Historical Association. Learn more at www.trochimczyk.net

JONATHAN VOS POST
Jonathan Vos Post is Co-Webmaster, Vice President, and Chief Information Officer of Magic Dragon Multimedia. He is a part-time professor at five colleges and universities in Southern California, teaching astronomy, computer science, English composition, mathematics, and physics. Vos Post's writings have appeared in numerous publications, and he has also appeared in broadcasts with notable science fiction writers. Vos Post has also won literary awards and been published in the *Nebula Awards Anthology, 1989*.

LORI WALL-HOLLOWAY
A wife, mother, and proud grandmother of nine grandchildren, Wall-Holloway lives in the San Gabriel Valley of California, where her poetry has appeared in several publications, including the *San Gabriel Valley Poetry Quarterly* and the annual anthologies, *Poetry and Cookies*. She served on this anthology's Selection Committee.

JACQUELYN BELLARD WILSON
A retired educator, Wilson's career included pre-school, elementary, and university teaching. She has embraced poetry as a means to communicate the emotions of heart, the perceptions of mind, and the attributes of soul, which make her whole. She began writing poetry at the age of seven. A previously published author, she is dedicated to continued growth. Wilson has lived in Pasadena with her husband for almost 37 years.

**Franklin D. Murdock passed away one month before publication of this anthology. He was a dear friend and inspiration to many of us. We honor his memory.

www.ingramcontent.com/pod-product-compliance
Lightning Source LLC
Chambersburg PA
CBHW022154260626
47155CB00018B/1875